Kingston Ontario Book 6 in Colour Photos, Saving Our History One Photo at a Time

Photography
by Barbara Raué
2016

Series Name:
Cruising Ontario

Book 145: Kingston Book 6

Cover photo: King Street West, Page 12

Series Name: Cruising Ontario
Saving Our History One Photo at a Time
in colour photos

Books Available in Alphabetical Order:

Aberfoyle, Acton, Alton, Ancaster, Arthur, Aylmer, Ayr, Bloomingdale, Brantford, Burlington, Caledon, Caledonia, Cambridge, Clifford, Conestogo, Delhi, Dorchester to Aylmer, Drayton, Drumbo, Dundas, Eden Mills, Elmira, Elora, Fergus, Guelph, Hagersville, Hamilton, Hanover, Harriston, Hespeler, Jarvis, Kitchener, Linwood, Listowel, London, Lucknow, Mono, Mount Forest, Neustadt, New Hamburg, Niagara-on-the-Lake, Oakville, Orangeville, Orillia, Owen Sound, Palmerston, Peterborough, Port Elgin, Preston, Rockwood, Seaforth, Sheffield, Shelburne, Simcoe, Southampton, St. Jacobs, St. Thomas, Stoney Creek, Stratford, Tillsonburg, Waterdown, Waterford, Waterloo, Wellesley, Wingham

Other Books by Barbara Raue

Coins of Gold

Arrows, Indians and Love

The Life and Times of Barbara
Volume 1: Inventions That Have Enhanced My Life
Volume 2: Entertainment That I Have Enjoyed
Volume 3: East Coast Trips
Volume 4: Olympics Have Always Intrigued Me
Volume 5: Wonders of the World
Volume 6: Caribbean Cruises We Have Enjoyed
Volume 7: Animals
Volume 8: Storms and Other Major Disasters in My Lifetime
Volume 9: Wars, Terrorist Attacks and Major Disasters

The Cromwell Family Book

Laura Secord Discovered

Daddy Where Are You?

Visit Barbara's website to view all of her books
http://barbararaue.ca

Kingston is located where the St. Lawrence River meets Lake Ontario and the Rideau Canal. It is a historic city midway between Toronto and Montreal. Kingston was the first capital of the Province of Canada. Kingston is nicknamed the "*Limestone City*" because of the many heritage buildings constructed using local limestone.

During the War of 1812, Kingston was the base for the Lake Ontario division of the Great Lakes British naval fleet, which engaged in a vigorous arms race with the American fleet based at Sackets Harbor, New York for control of Lake Ontario. Fortifications and other defensive structures were built. In the 1840s, the Upper Canadian government built Fort Henry and a series of distinctive Martello towers to guard the entrance to the Rideau Canal, the shipyard on Point Frederick, and the harbor. All still exist, and Fort Henry is a popular tourist attraction. The nearby village of Barriefield, overlooking the Cataraqui River was settled in the 1830s, and is now a well-preserved historical neighborhood.

The Kingston Penitentiary which opened on June 1, 1835 was Canada's oldest reformatory prison. Its layout – an imposing front gate leading to a cross-shaped cellblock with workshops to the rear – was the model for other federal prisons for more than a century. It is Classical architecture in local stone.

Kingston Penitentiary represented a significant departure from the way society had dealt with its criminals. Previously, jails were used primarily as places to hold convicts awaiting execution, banishment, or public humiliation. The penitentiary imposed a severe regime designed to reform the inmate through reflection, hard work, and the fear of punishment. Inmates lived in small cells but worked together from dawn to dusk under a rigidly enforced code of silence. Kingston Penitentiary stands as a symbol of this country's commitment to maintaining law and order.

Table of Contents

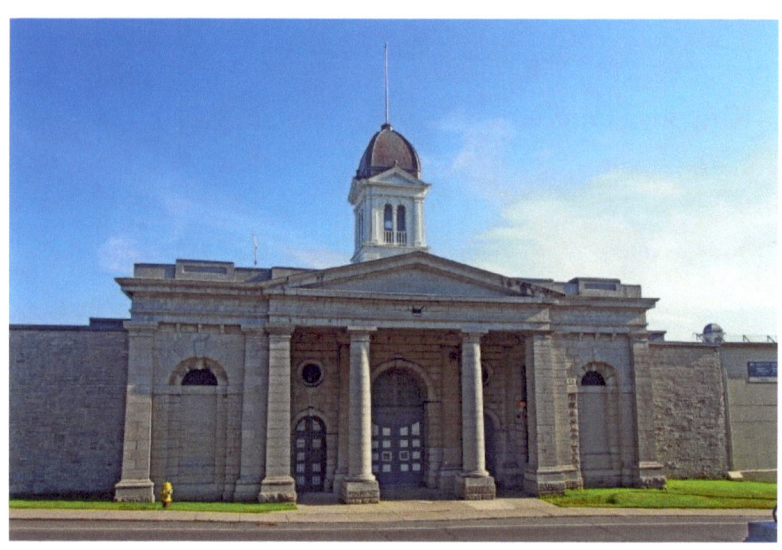

555 King Street West - Kingston Penitentiary – Men's – in operation as a prison from 1835-1985

Neo-Classical architecture made from local stone – constructed 1843-1846 - large central arched entranceway with two smaller arched pedestrian walkways to either side; two freestanding columns frame the main arched entrance; an entablature, a paneled parapet, and a pediment cap give the North Lodge its temple like appearance. The tall helm crested lantern tower is the highest point of the building. To either side of this composition are projecting attached pavilions featuring a blind window within a double recessed panel - voussoirs and keystones

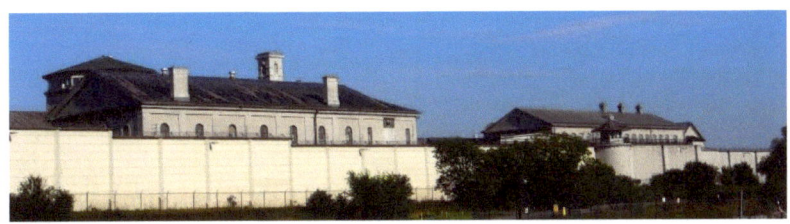

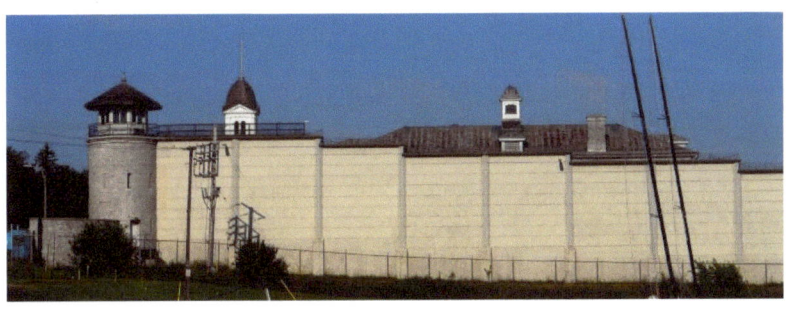

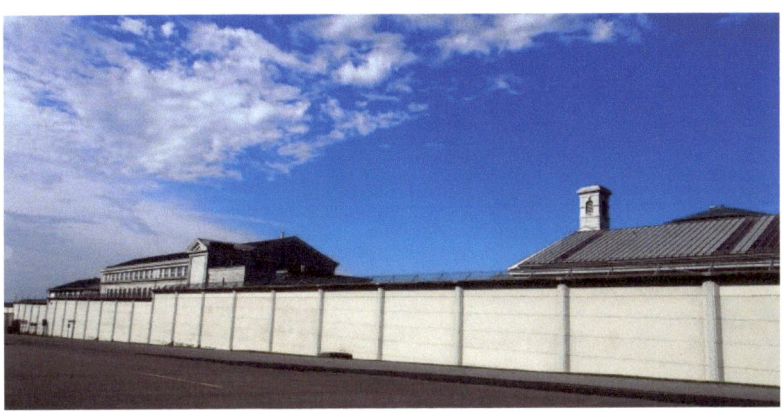

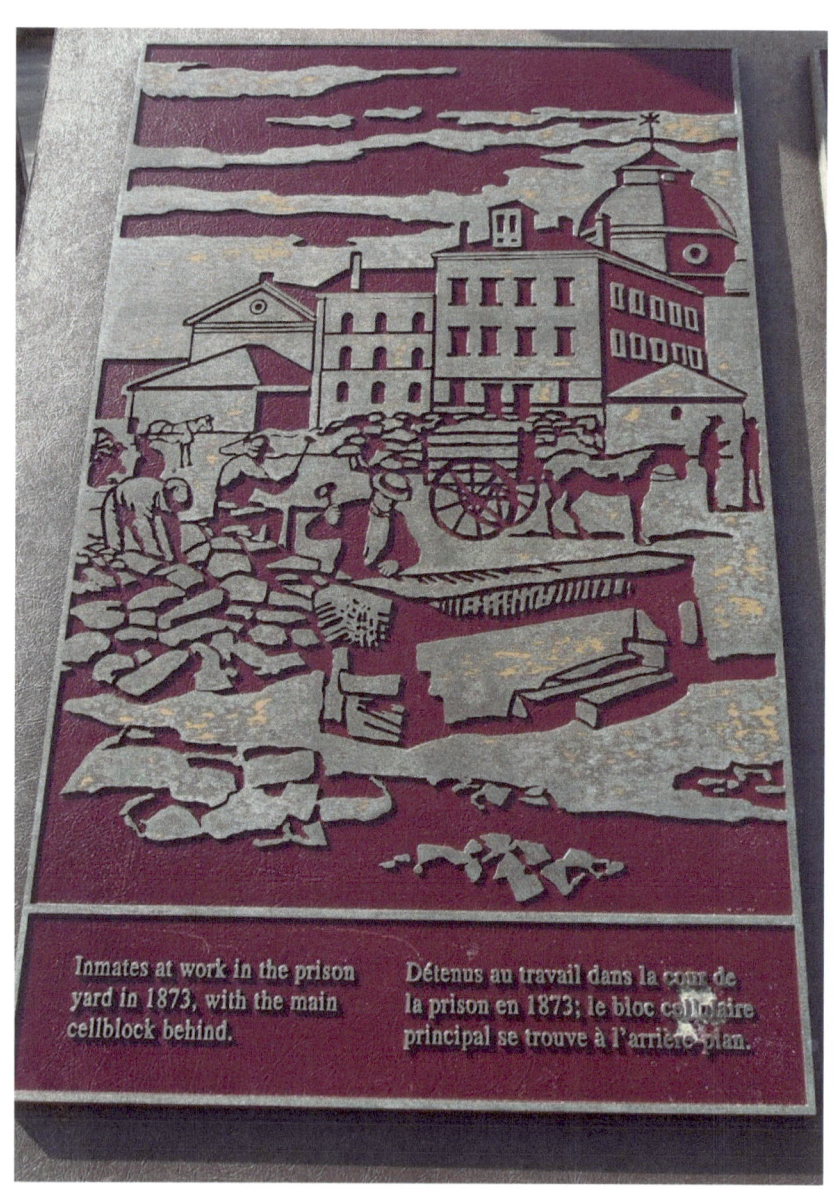

Inmates at work in the prison yard in 1873, with the main cellblock behind.

Détenus au travail dans la cour de la prison en 1873; le bloc cellulaire principal se trouve à l'arrière-plan.

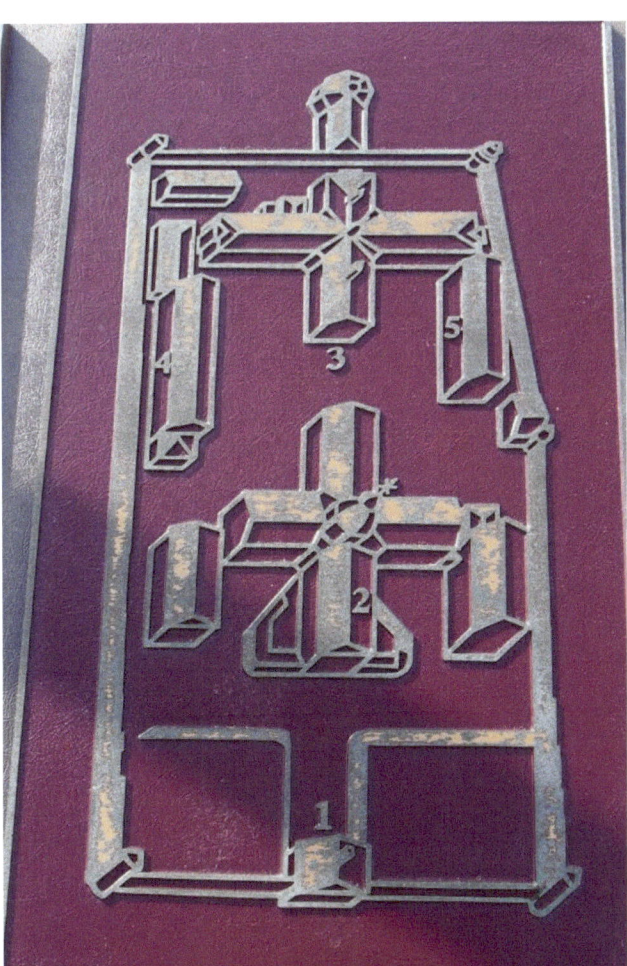

An aerial view of the penitentiary in 1895. The major buildings were:
1. North Gate
2. Main Cellblock
3. South Shops
4. Prison of Isolation
5. Asylum

Vue aérienne du pénitencier en 1895. Les principaux bâtiments étaient:
1. la barrière du nord
2. le bloc cellulaire principal
3. les ateliers du sud
4. la prison d'isolement
5. l'asile

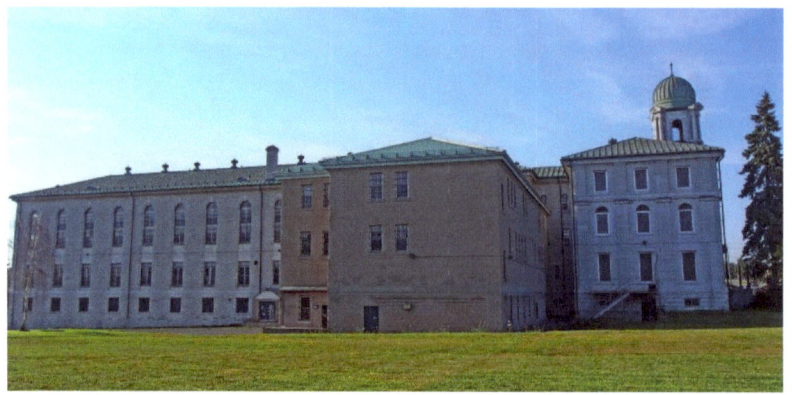

Women's Penitentiary – shallow hipped roof, cupola

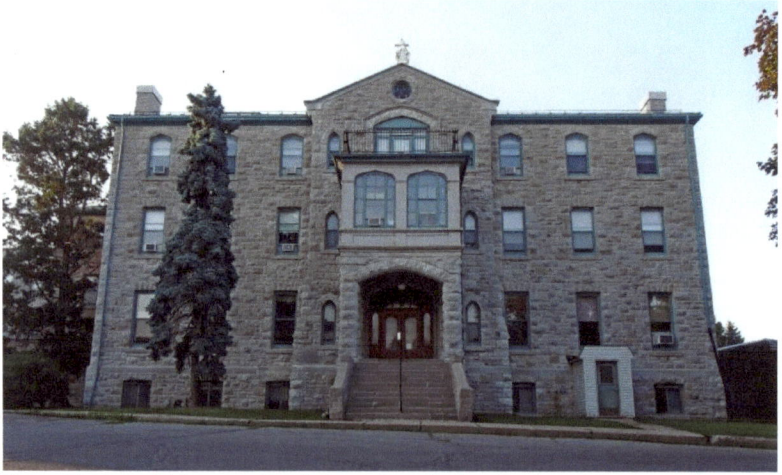

King Street West – St. Mary's of the Lake Hospital - 1908
(Corner stone: Orphanage of the Novitiate and of the Sisters of
the House of Providence) - In 1910, orphans from Providence
Manor were moved to St. Mary's of the Lake which remained
an orphanage until the 1940s – three storeys, frontispiece

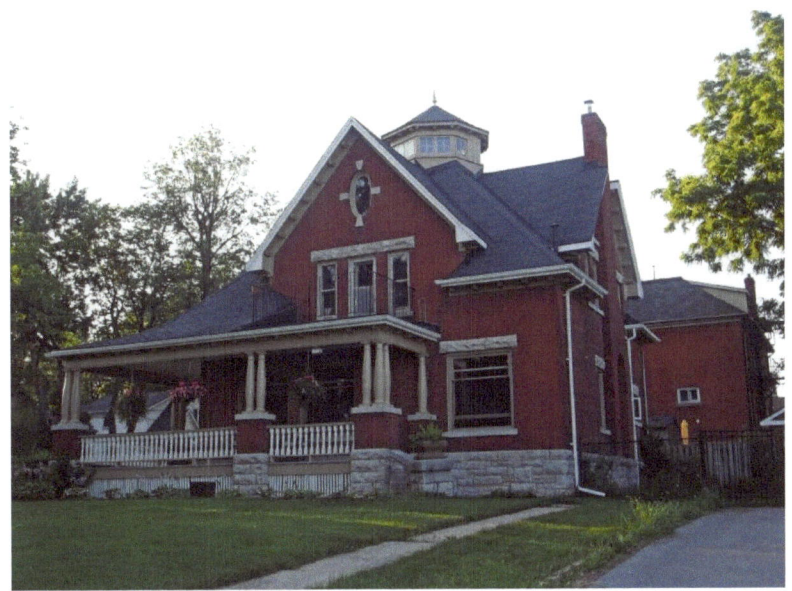

371 King Street West – belvedere, second floor balcony

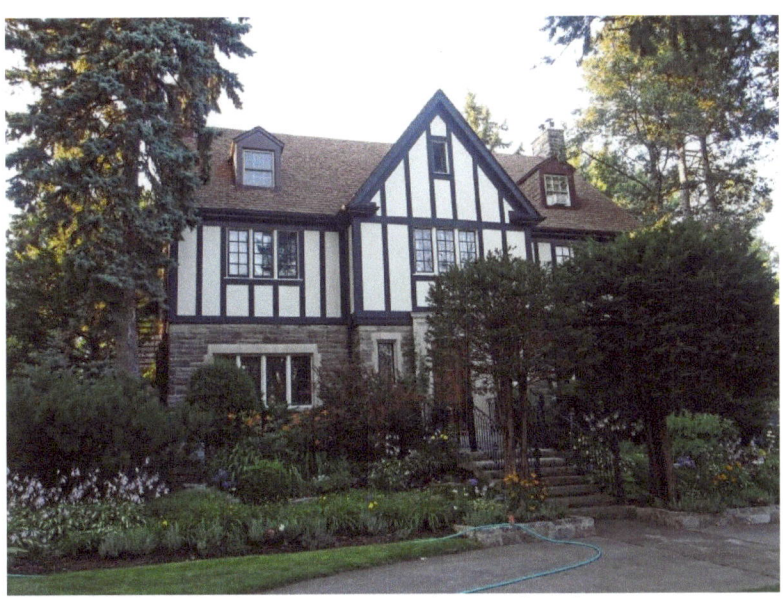

King Street West – Tudor style, dormers

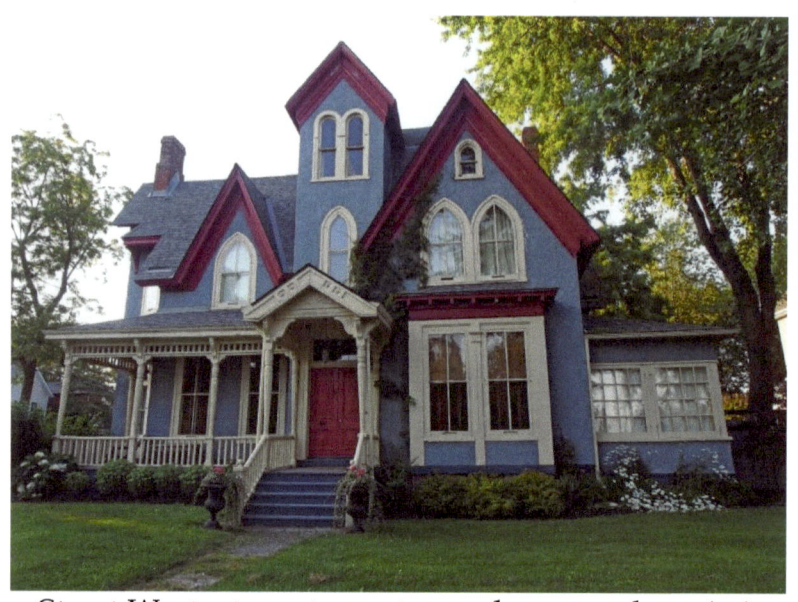

King Street West – two-storey tower, lancet and semi-circular windows, transom window above door

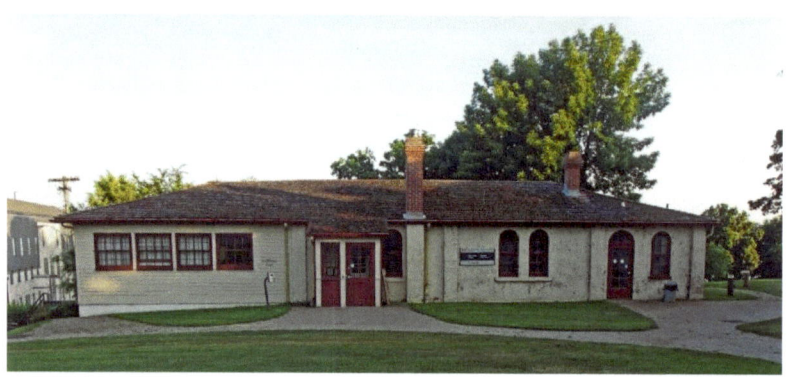

440 King Street West - The St. Helen's Complex, Red Cross Lodge – stuccoed, brick building with a hipped roof is set into the grade of a hill fronting Lake Ontario. Its simple, classically-inspired appearance is distinguished by large round-arched windows, pilasters and tall chimneys. Two wings project from the east and west sides of the building.

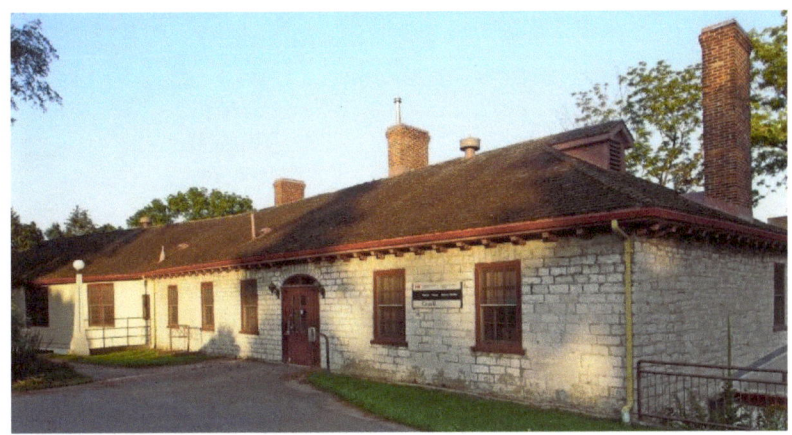

St. Helen's Complex - Morton's Lodge – stone - James Morton, a prominent figure in the early history of Kingston and Canada, was the owner of the adjoining brewery complex and a local industrialist

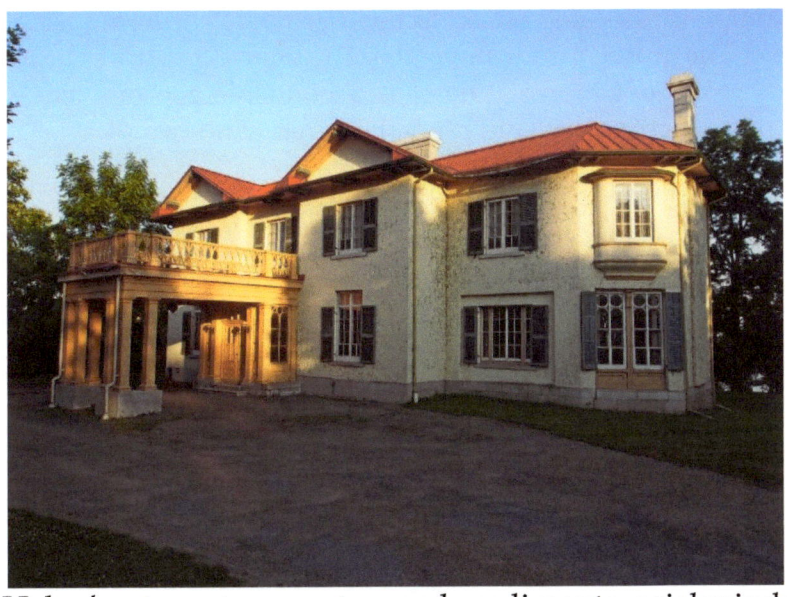

St. Helen's – two storeys, stuccoed, pediments, oriel window, and tall chimneys, impressive pillared entrance with second floor balcony

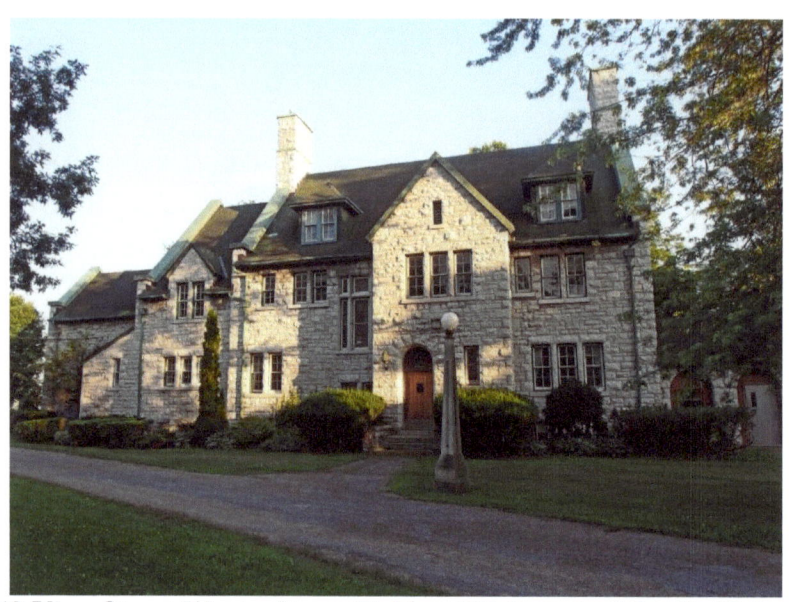

462 King Street West - Stone Gables, 1924, part of the St. Helen's Complex, is located on landscaped grounds bordering Lake Ontario. The grand, Tudor Revival, stone building features a steeply pitched gable roof, a projecting gabled frontispiece, prominent gable chimneys, and hipped dormer windows.

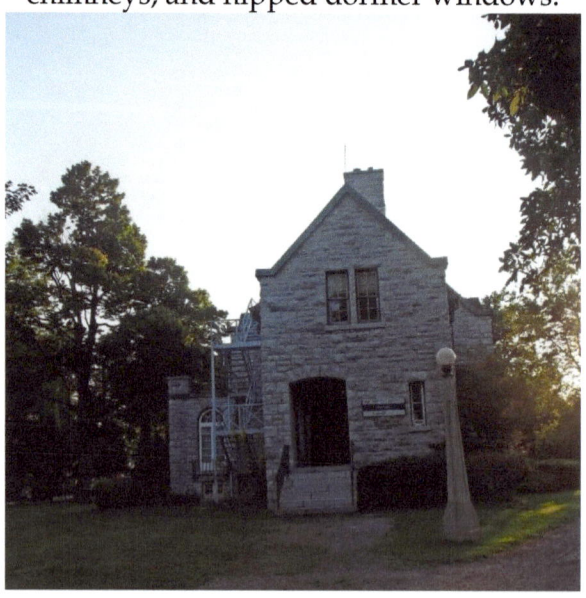

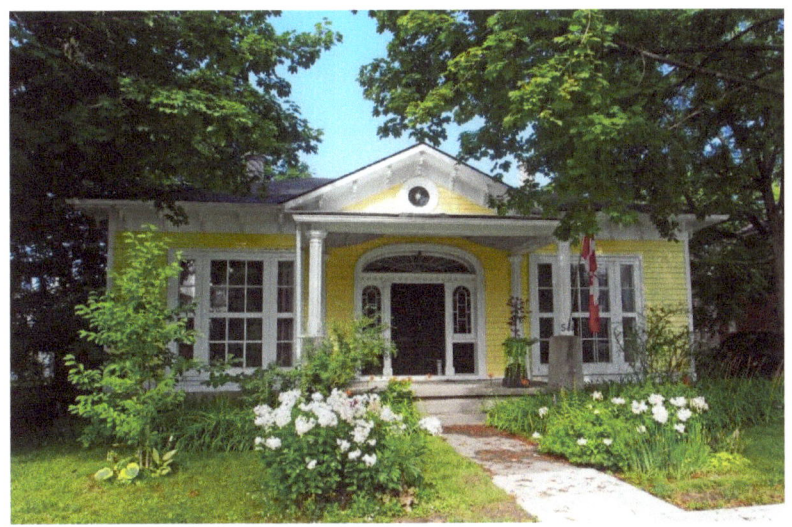

56 King Street West – Regency Cottage - pediment

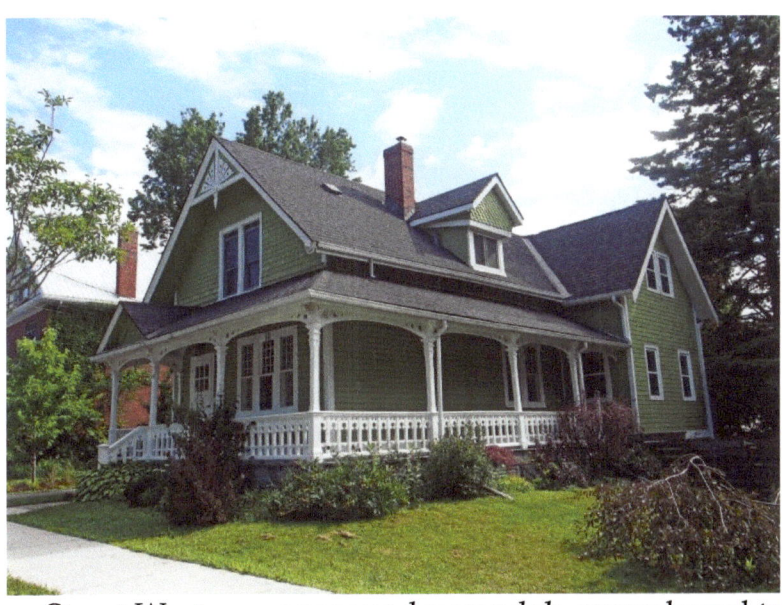

King Street West – wraparound verandah, verge board trim
on gable, dormer

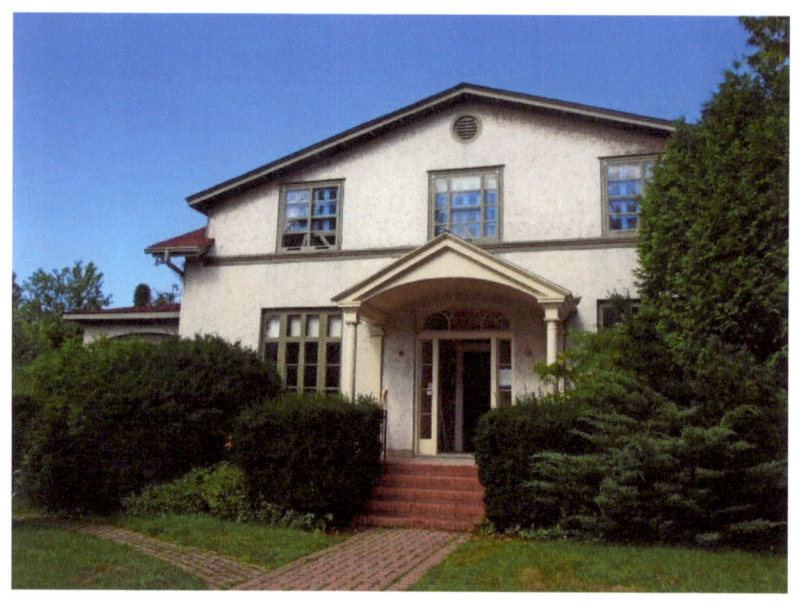

King Street West – stucco, pillared entrance, sidelights and transom window above door

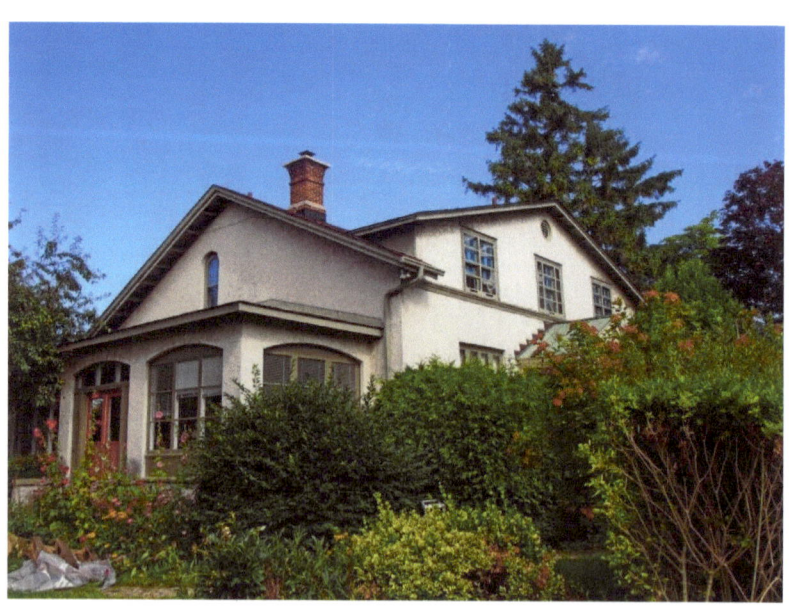

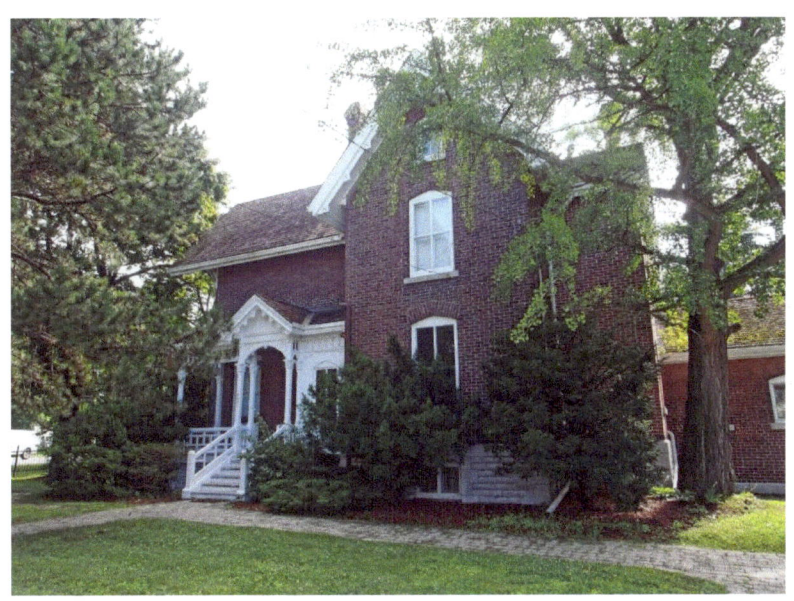

77 King Street West

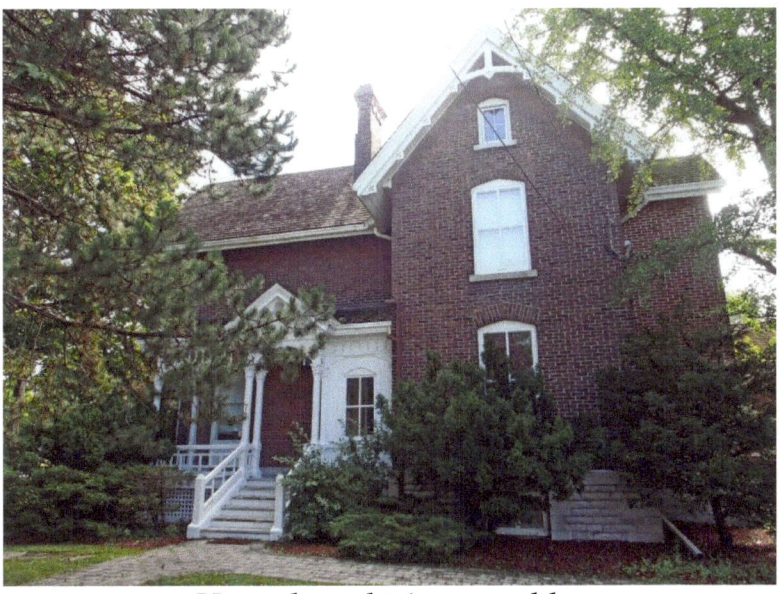

Verge board trim on gable

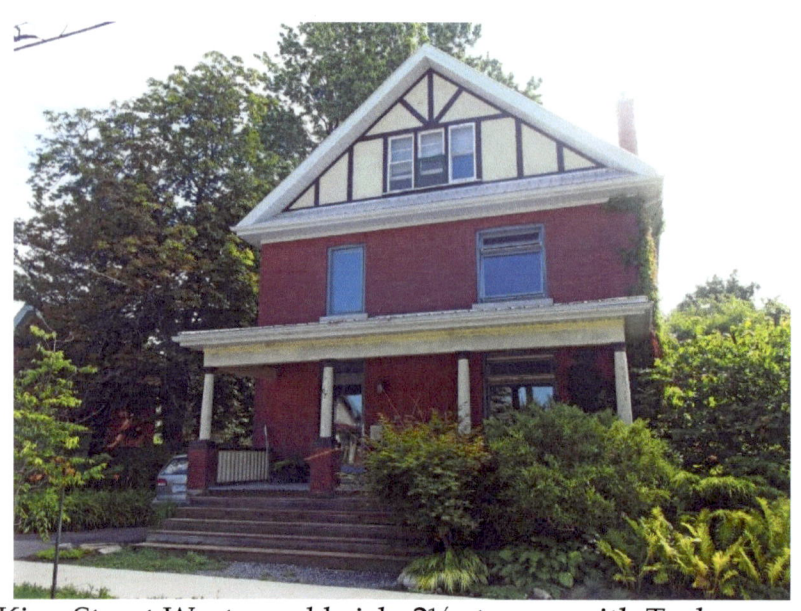

67 King Street West – red brick, 2½ storeys with Tudor accents on gable

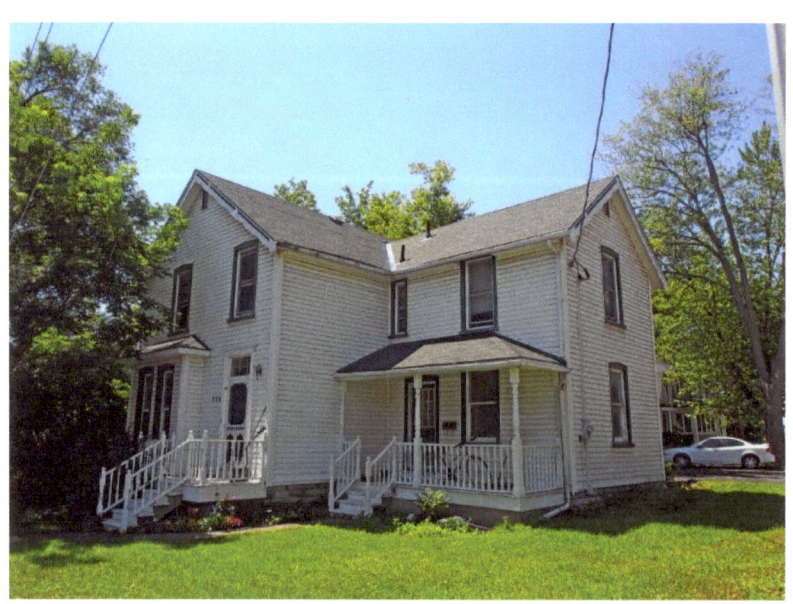

114 Livingstone Avenue

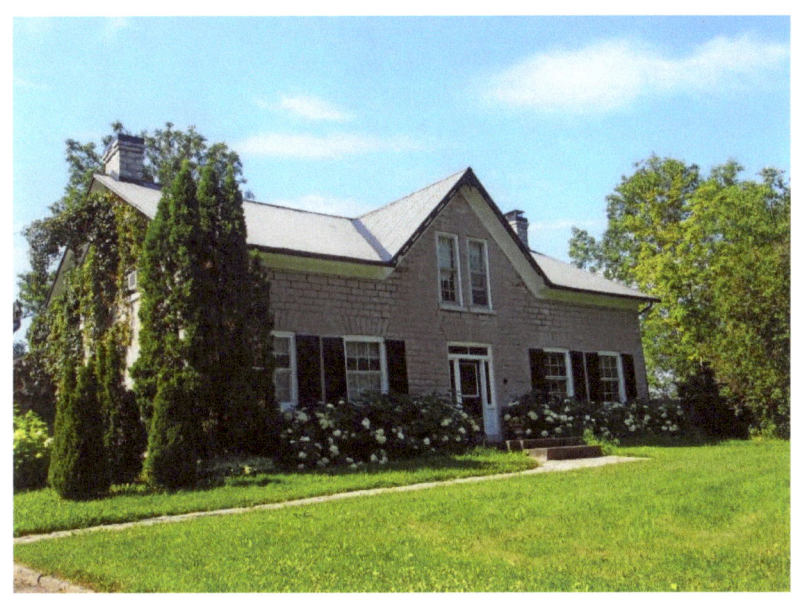

1345 Woodbine Road

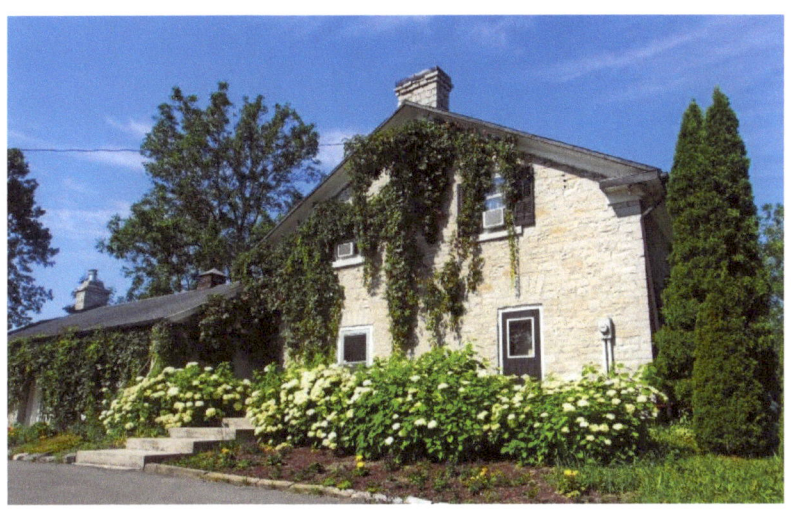

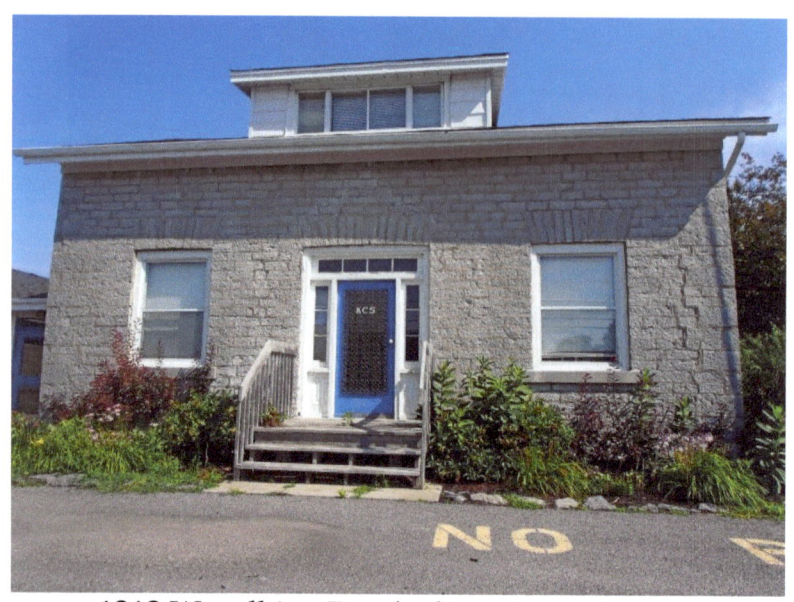

1212 Woodbine Road – limestone, dormer

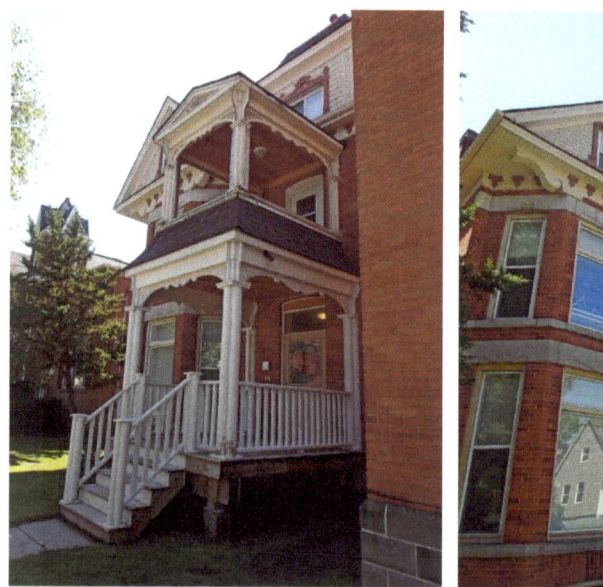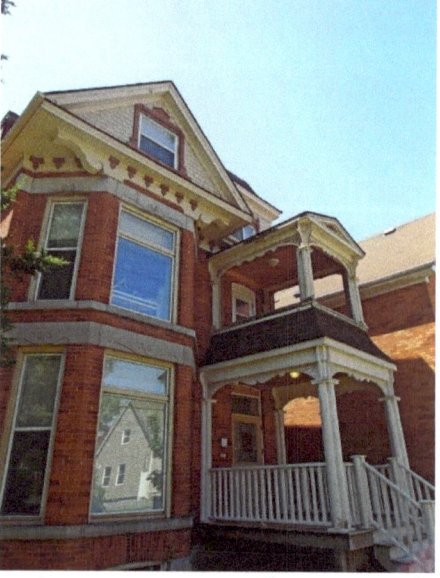

Union Street – wooden pillars on two-storey porches topped with pediment, decorative cornice, and two-storey tower-like bay topped with pediment

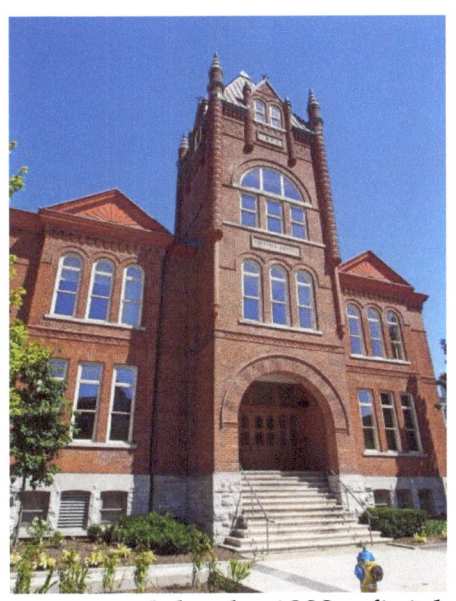

Union Street – Victoria School – 1892 – finials on 3½ storey tower, pediments, bevelled dentil moulding, semi-circular arched entry

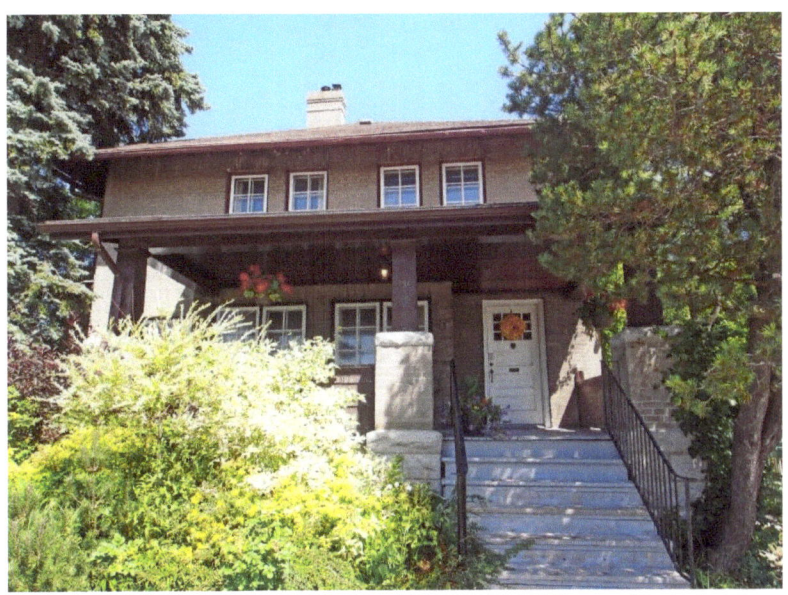

151 Union Street – two storeys, hipped roof

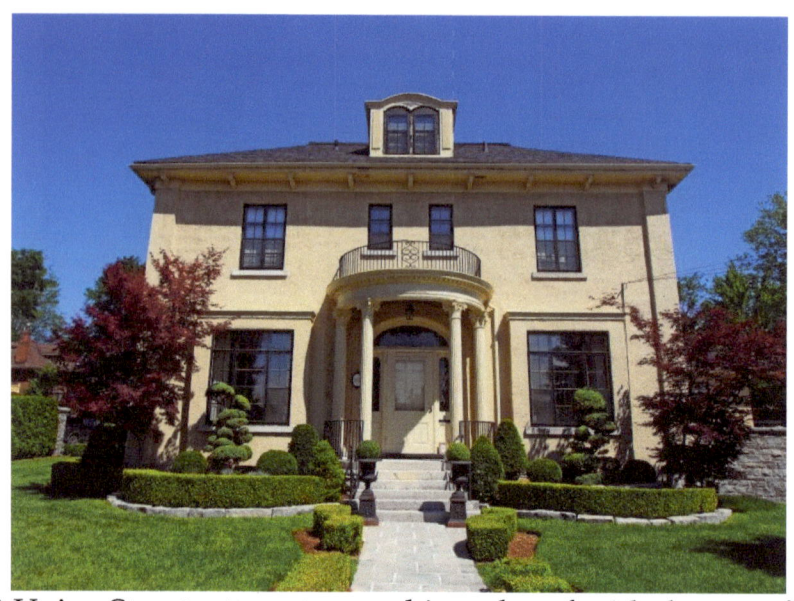

163 Union Street – two storeys, hipped roof with dormer, four Corinthian pillars supporting a semi-circular roof with balcony above, dentil moulding, sidelights and transom windows around door

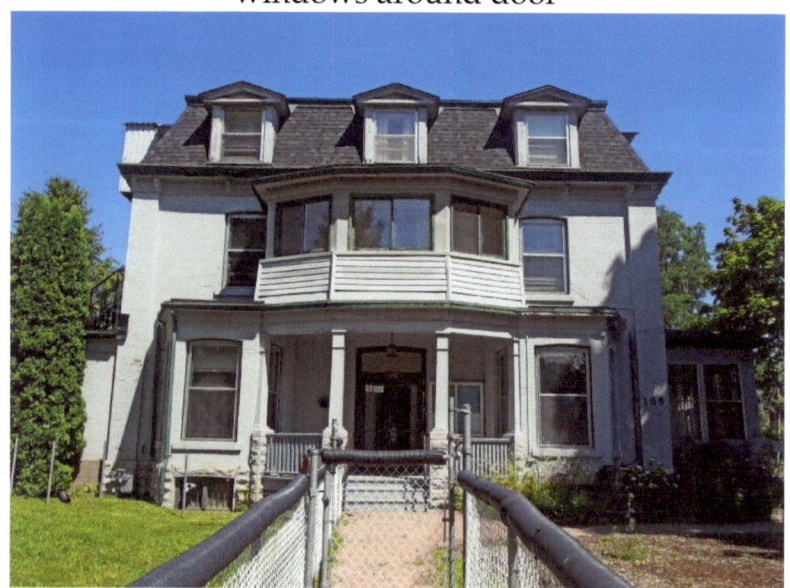

169 Union Street – Mansard-type roof with dormers

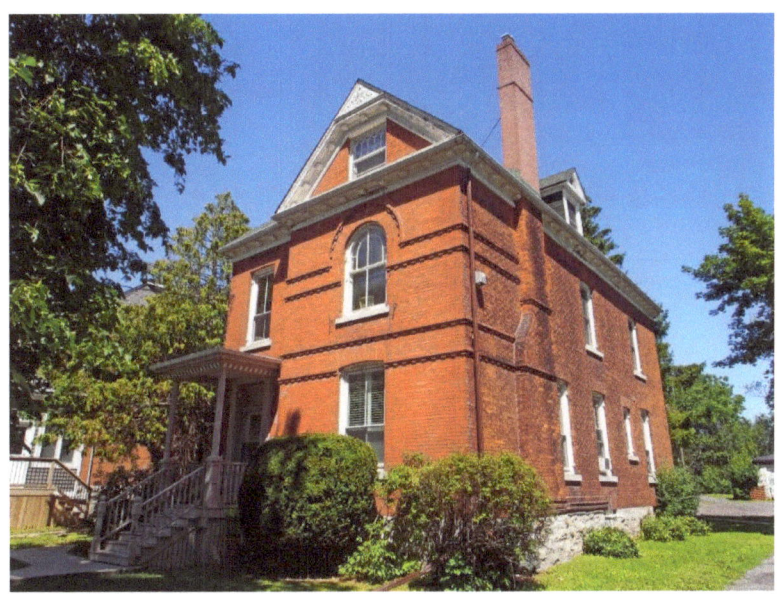

171 Union Street – two storey red brick with dormers, dentil moulding

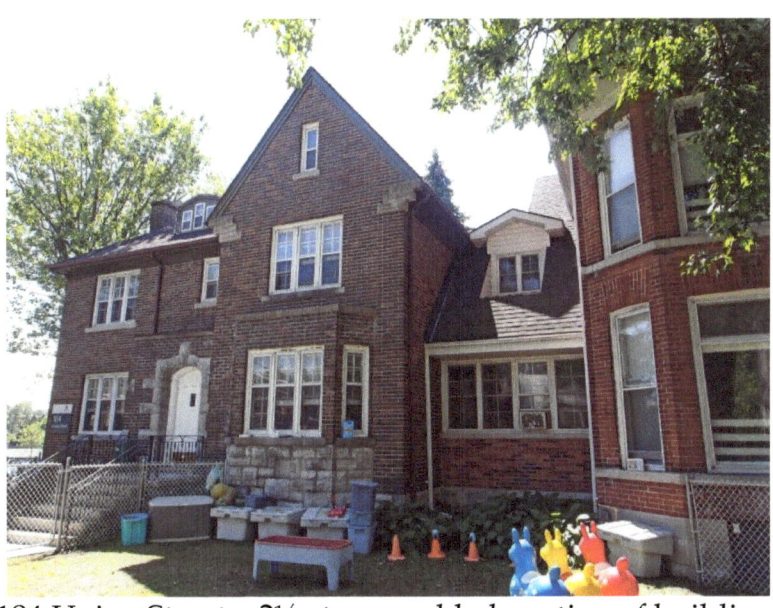

184 Union Street – 2½ storey gabled portion of building, dormer in each of one-storey and two-storey sections, quoining around door

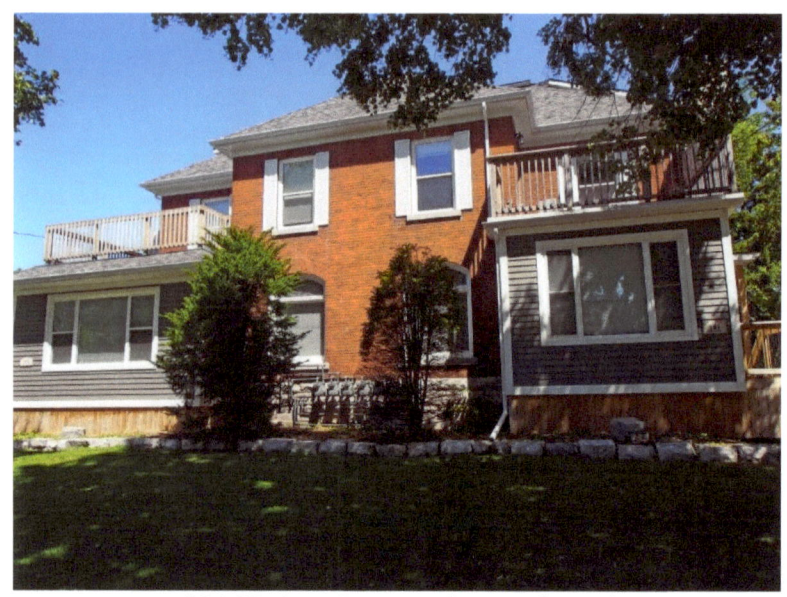

181 Union Street – hipped roof

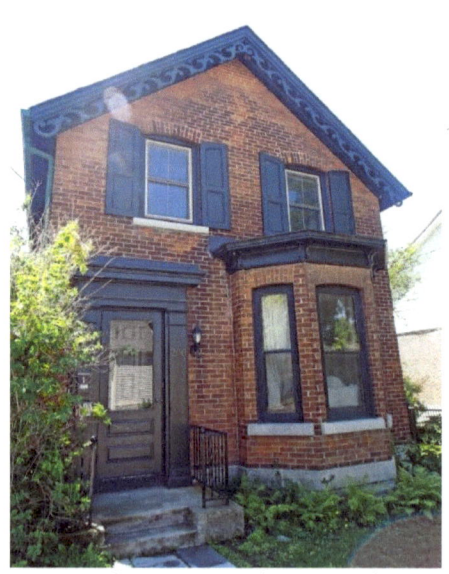

200 Union Street – Gothic Revival, verge board trim on gable, bay window

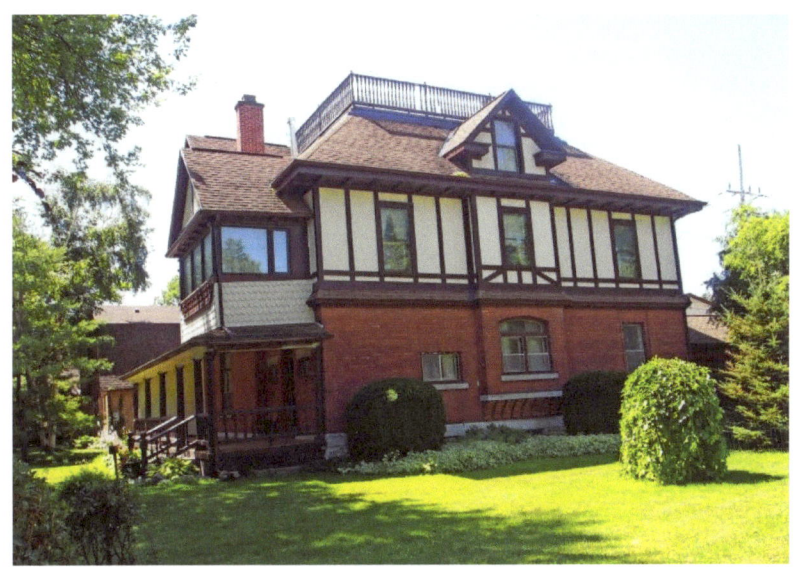

Union Street – Tudor style, cornice return on gabled dormer, rooftop balcony

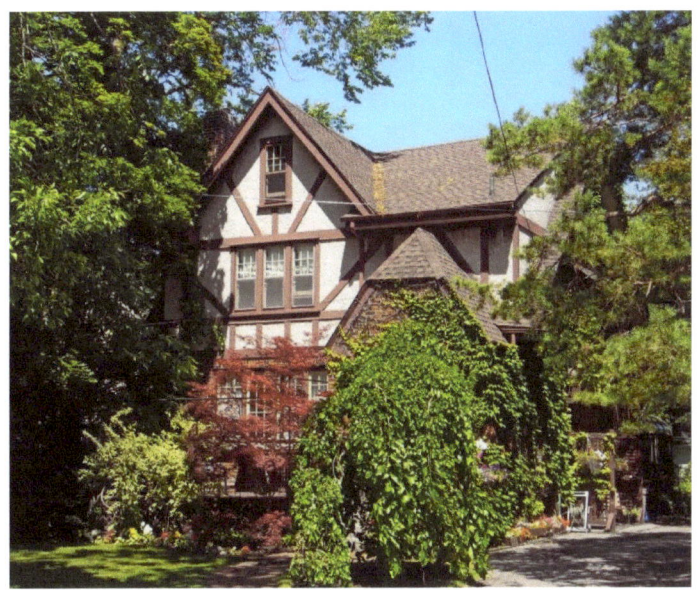

Union Street

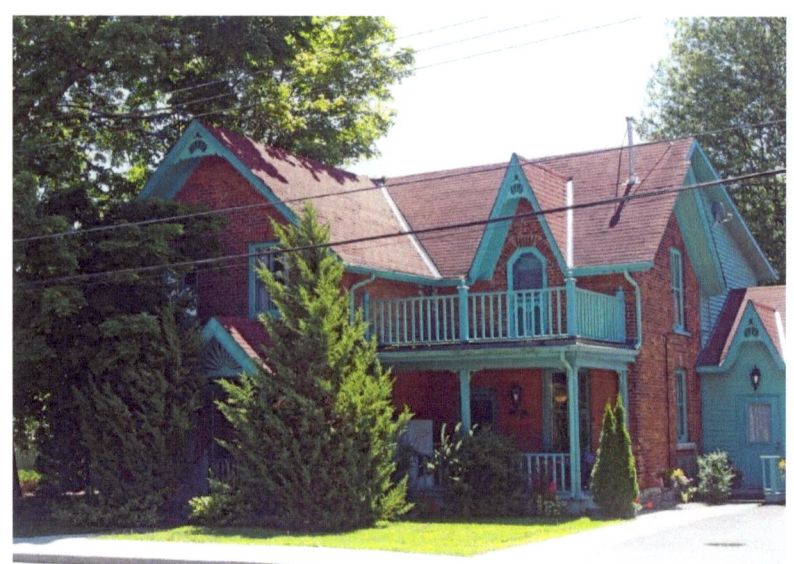

Union Street – Gothic Revival, trim on gables, second floor
balcony

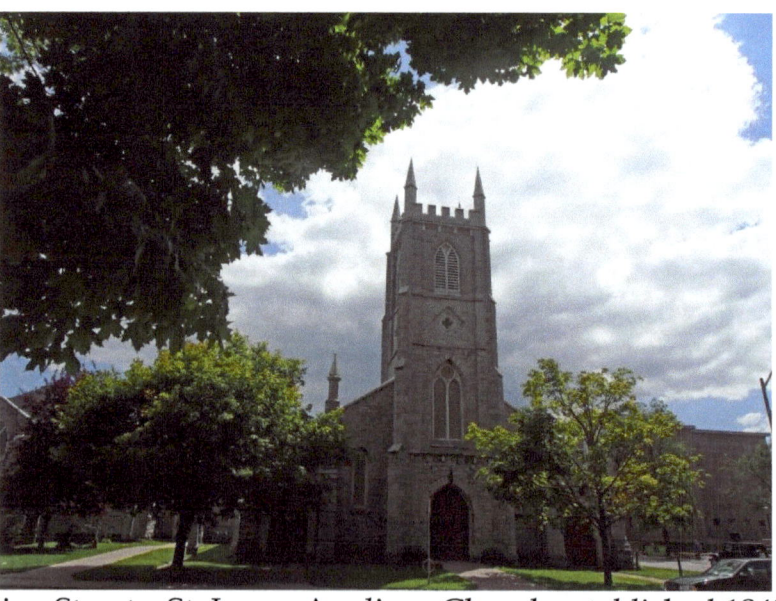

Union Street – St. James Anglican Church established 1843 –
Gothic Revival, lancet windows, crenelated tower, buttresses

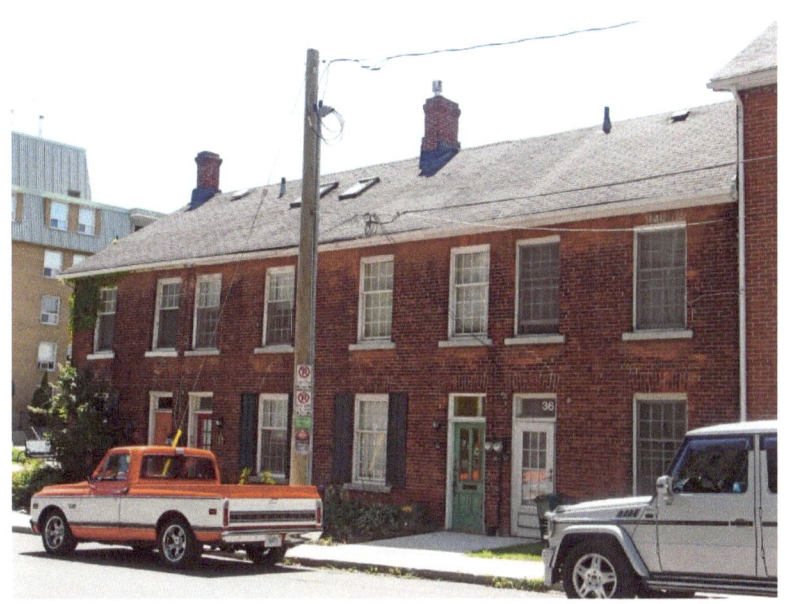

30-36 Lower Union Street – two-storey red brick, multi-paned sash windows, voussoirs

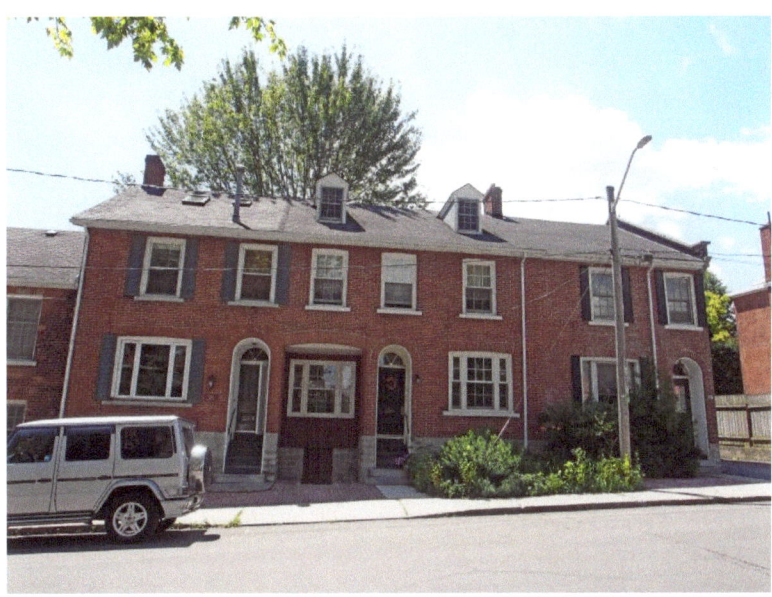

38-40 Lower Union Street – two-storey red brick, multi-paned sash windows, transom window, dormers in attic

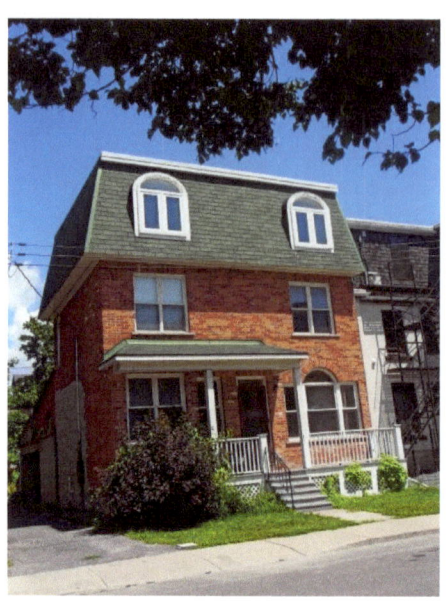

Lower Union Street - Mansard-type roof with dormers

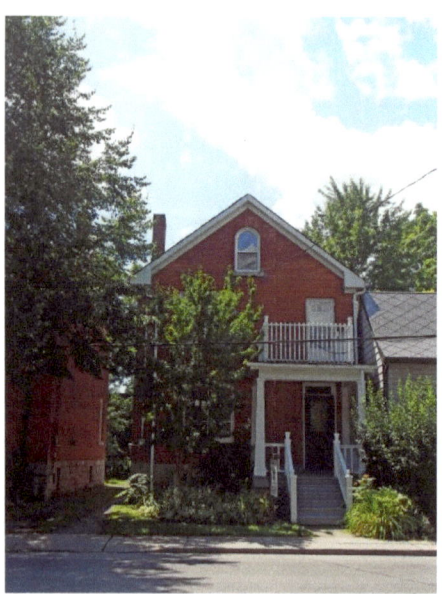

68 Lower Union Street - Gothic Revival

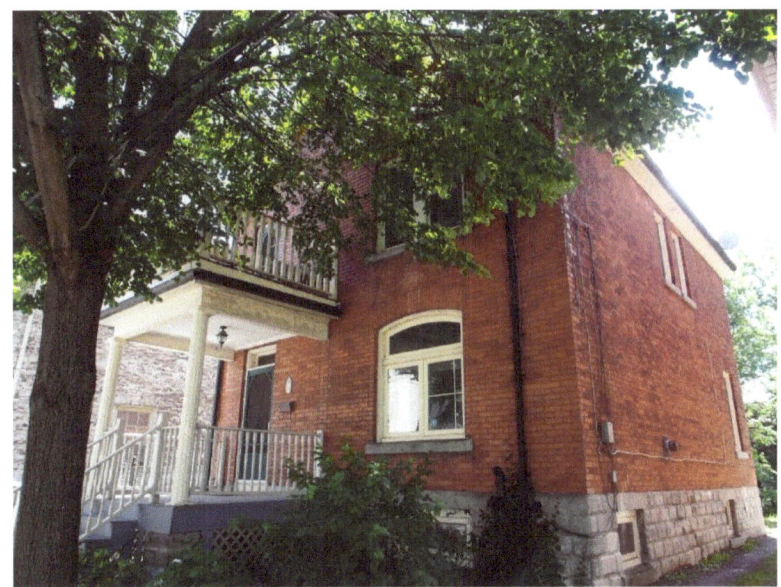

64 Lower Union Street – two-storey red brick, second floor balcony, transom window

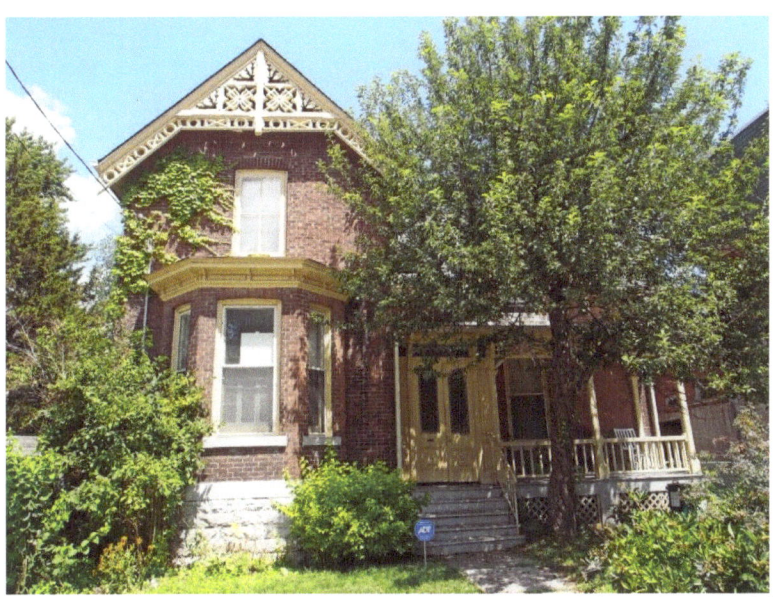

Lower Union Street – verge board trim and finial on gable, bay window

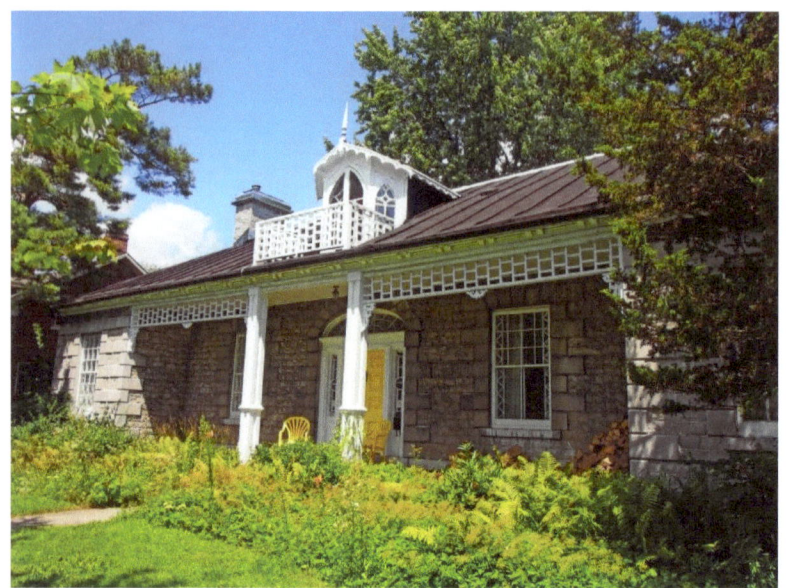

75 Lower Union Street – Charles Place – Regency Cottage built before 1832 – dormer and small upper porch added in 1840s – deeply recessed central porch, intricately designed doorway and sidelight windows with fancy borders

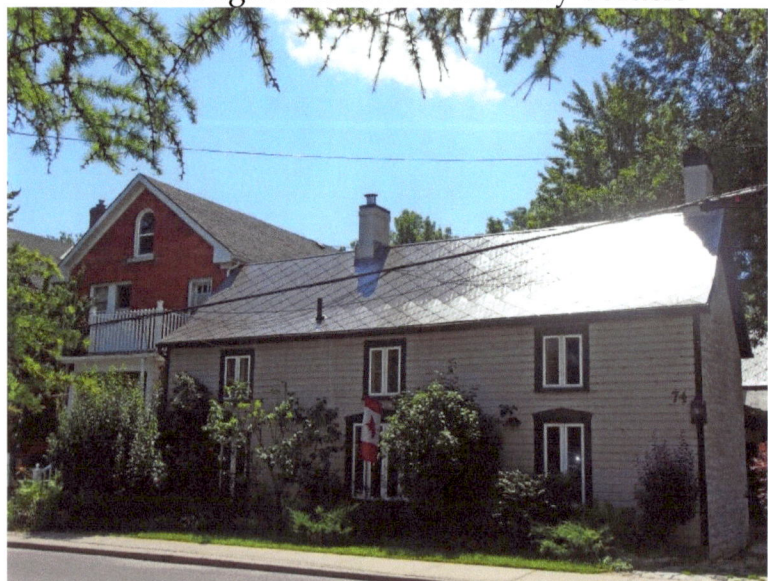

74 Lower Union Street – two storeys

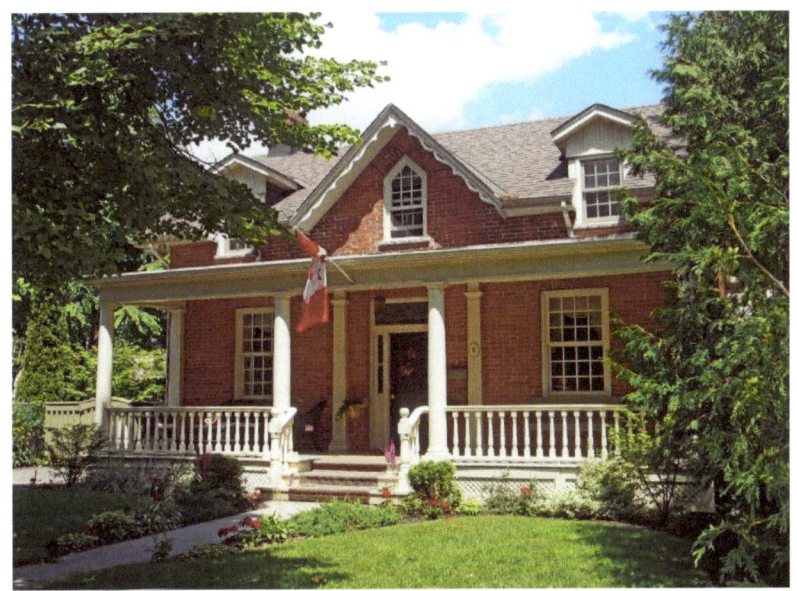

81 Lower Union Street – Gothic - 1½ storey brick cottage built
in 1875 – narrow sidelight windows, porch with Doric pillars –
carved wooden bargeboard on gable, dormers

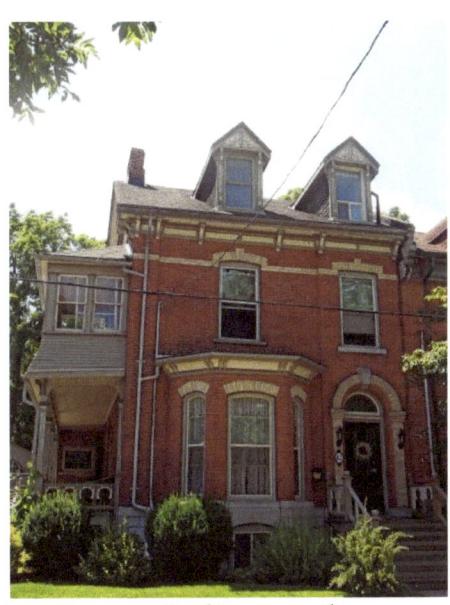

82 Lower Union Street - Italianate, dormers, bay window,
dichromatic brickwork, banding, cornice brackets

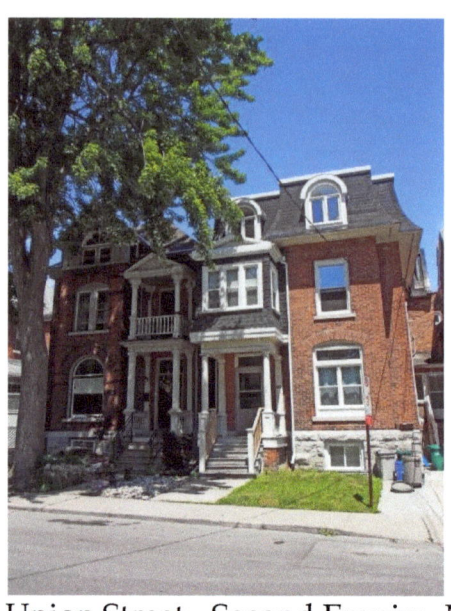

99-101 Lower Union Street - Second Empire, Mansard roof, dormers, two-storied pillared porches with pediment, transom windows above doors

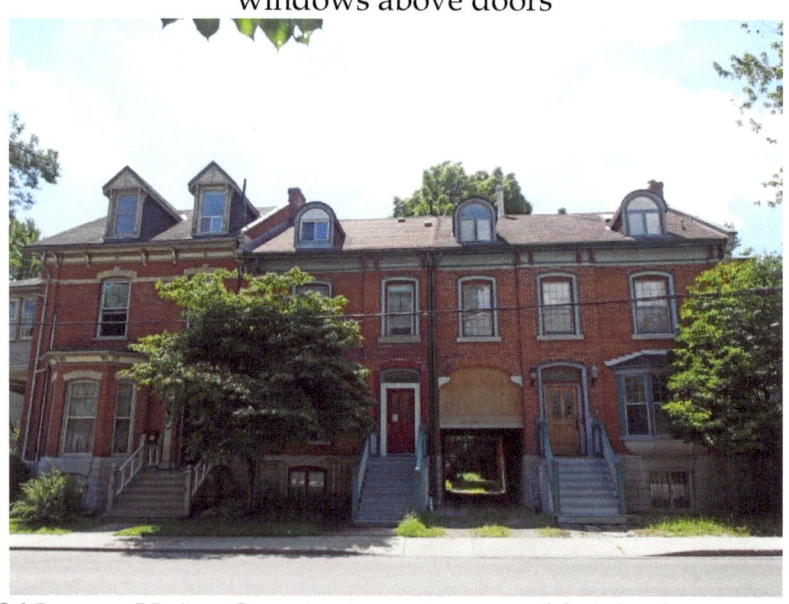

82-86 Lower Union Street – two storey red brick, dormers, bay windows

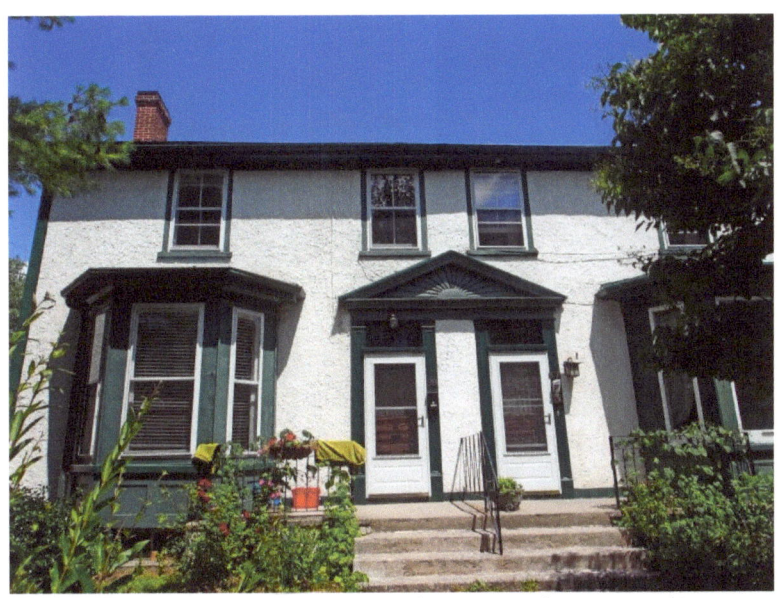
87-89 Lower Union Street – bay windows, pediment

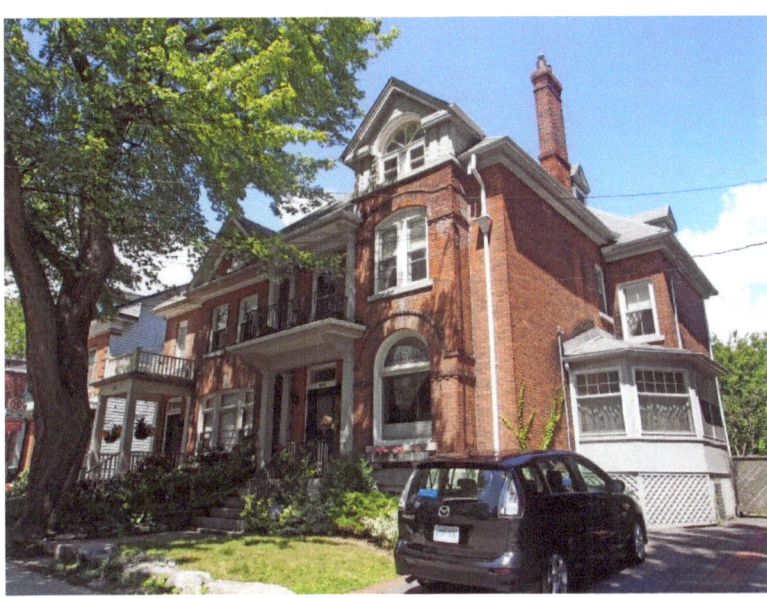
103 Lower Union Street – two-storey red brick, gabled dormer with cornice return, semi-circular arched window voussoirs, second floor balcony

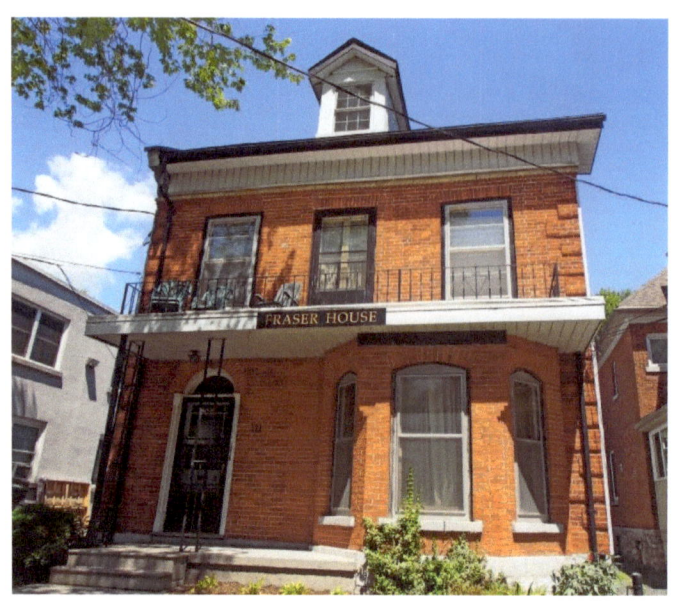

111 Lower Union Street – Fraser House – two-storey red brick, dormer, bay window, corner quoins, second floor balcony

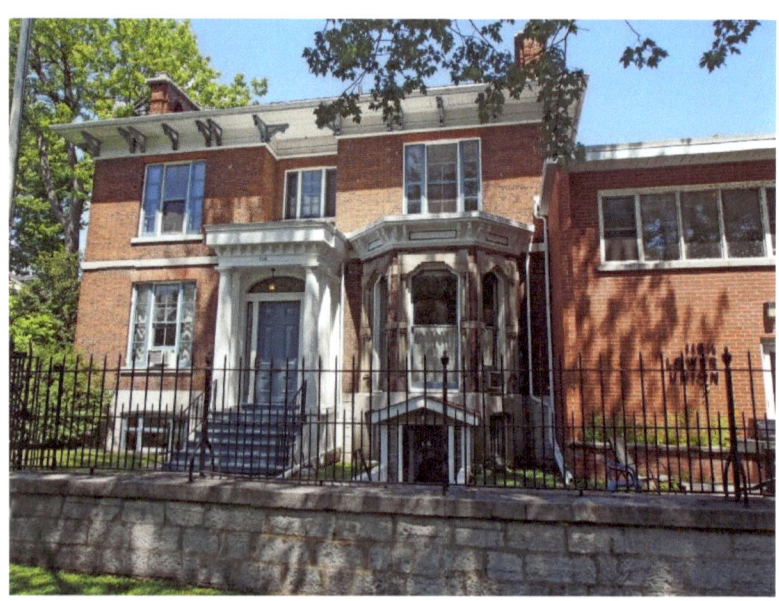

115 Lower Union Street – cornice brackets, banding, bay window, pillared entrance, sidelights and transom windows

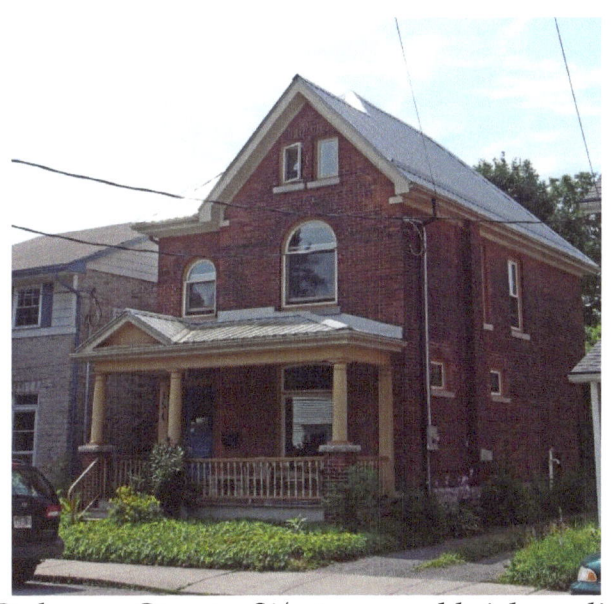

154 Ordnance Street – 2½ storey red brick, pediment

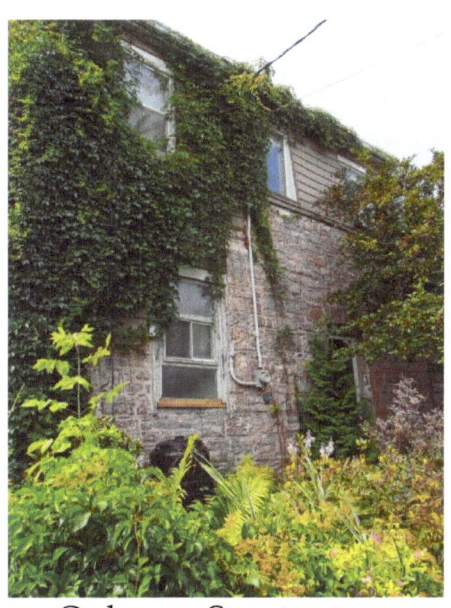

Ordnance Street - stone

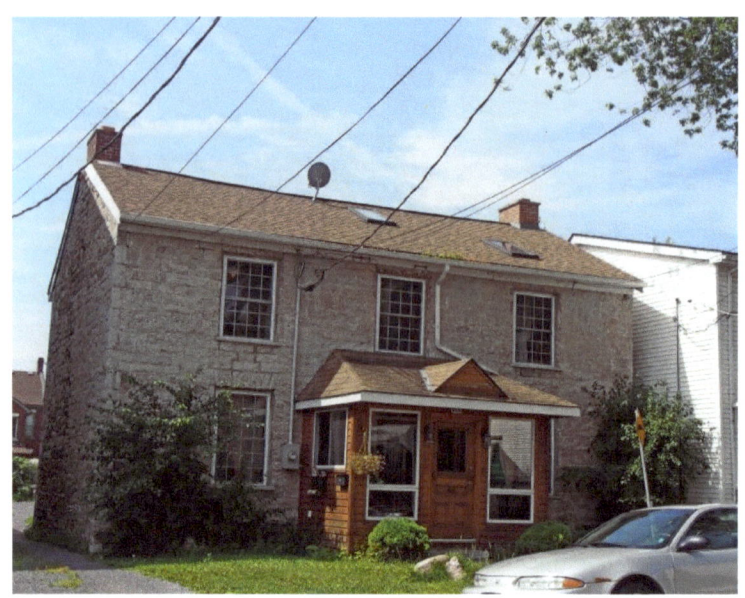

146 Ordnance Street – two storey stone, multi-paned windows

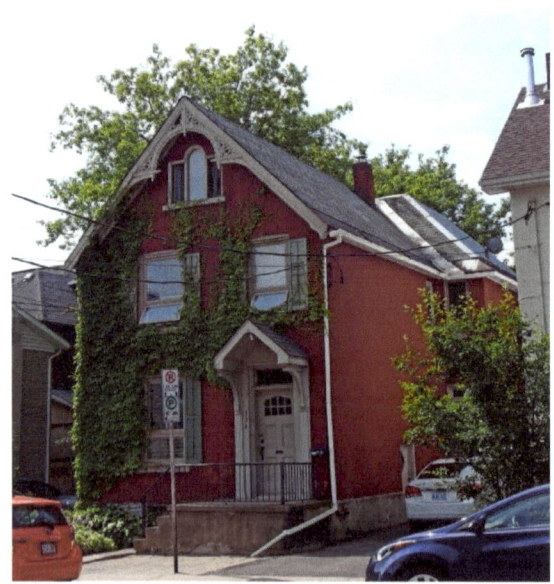

134 Ordnance Street – Gothic Revival - 2½ storey red brick,
verge board trim on gable

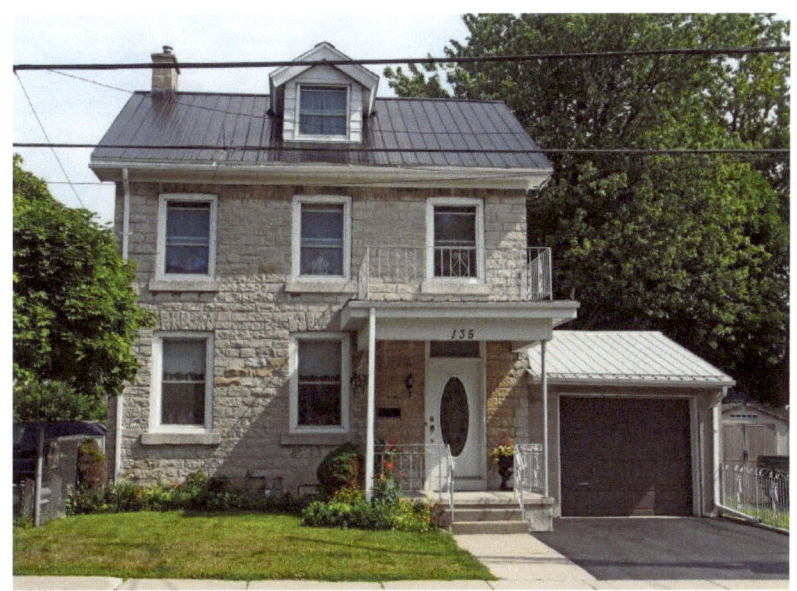

132 Ordnance Street – two storey limestone, dormer, second floor balcony, transom window

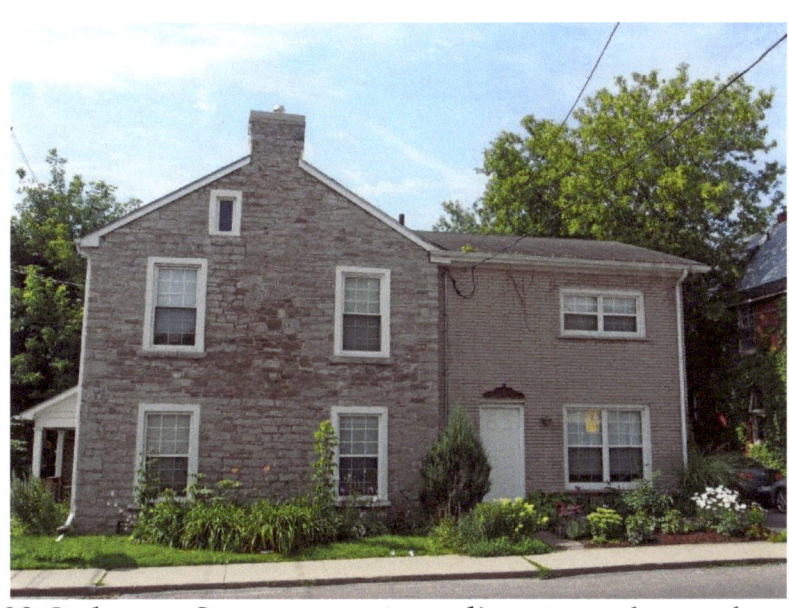

132 Ordnance Street – two storey limestone, 6-over-6 sash windows

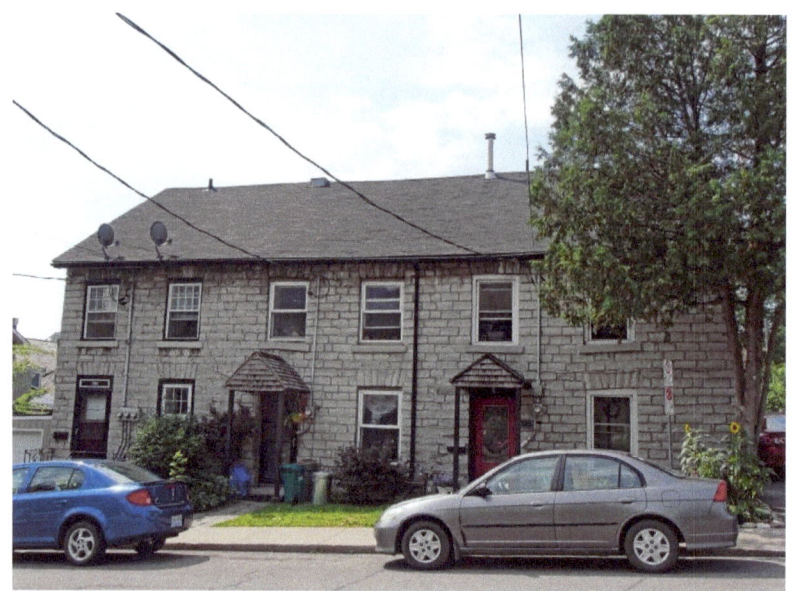

114-118 Ordnance Street – two storey limestone

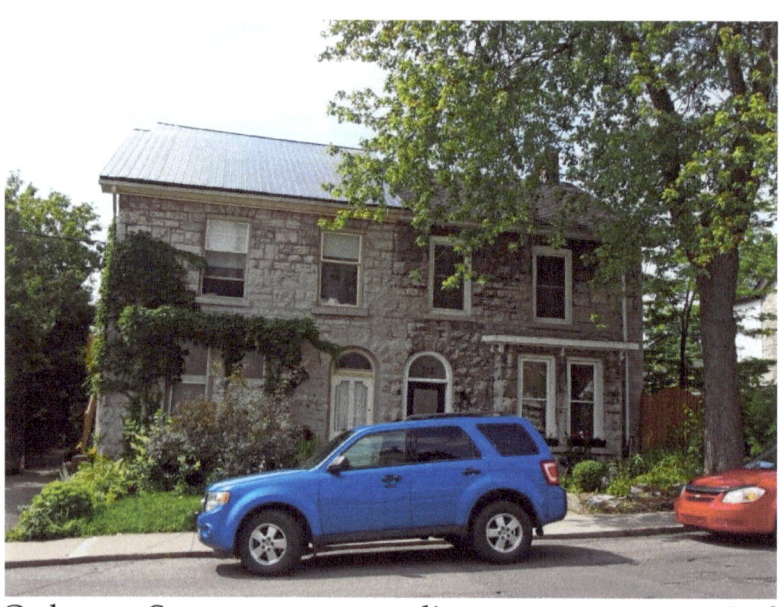

112 Ordnance Street – two storey limestone, transom windows

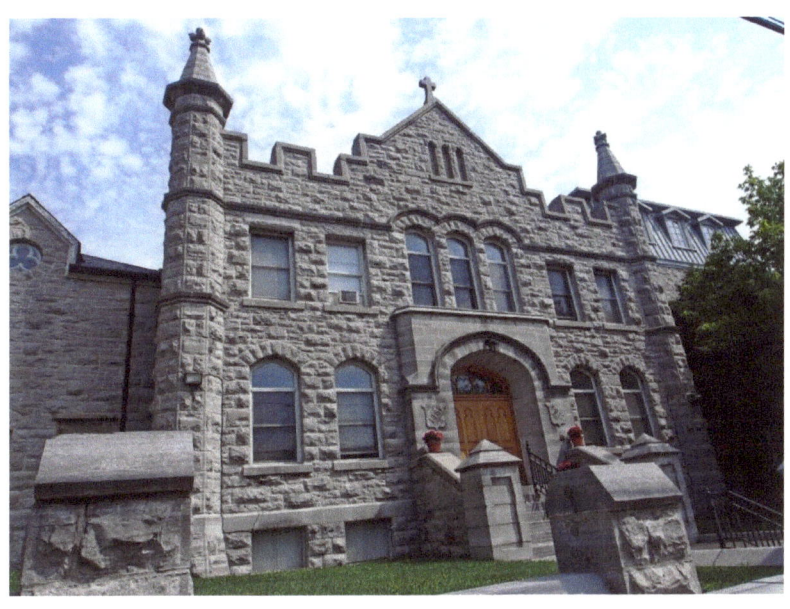

Ordnance Street – Institute of the Sisters of Charity – House of
Providence – 1838 – Romanesque style, Jacobean gable,
crenelated roofline, finials

Its heritage is rooted in the creativity and spirituality of
Vincent de Paul and Louise de Marillac, in the willingness of
Emilie Gamelin to risk and trust in Providence, in the
responsiveness of the Montreal Sisters of Providence to the
call of Bishop E.J. Horan, the ecclesiastical founder, and in the
courage and pioneer spirit of Catherine McKinley, the first
general superior and proclaimed Kingston foundress, and the
original members of the Kingston community

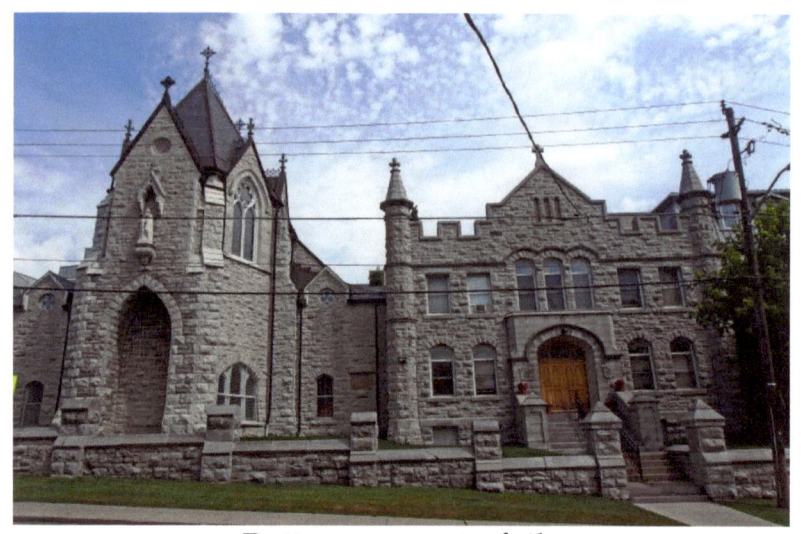

Buttresses, quatrefoils

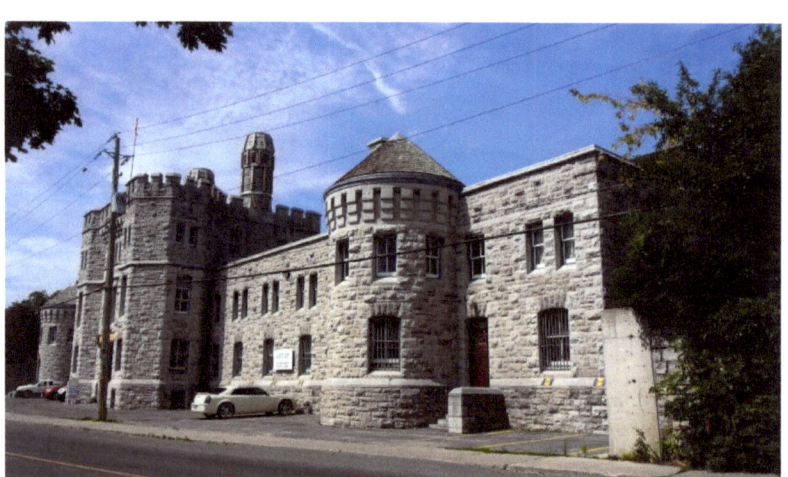

100 Montreal Street – Armouries – c. 1901 – houses Kingston's
militia unit, the Princess of Wales' Own Regiment

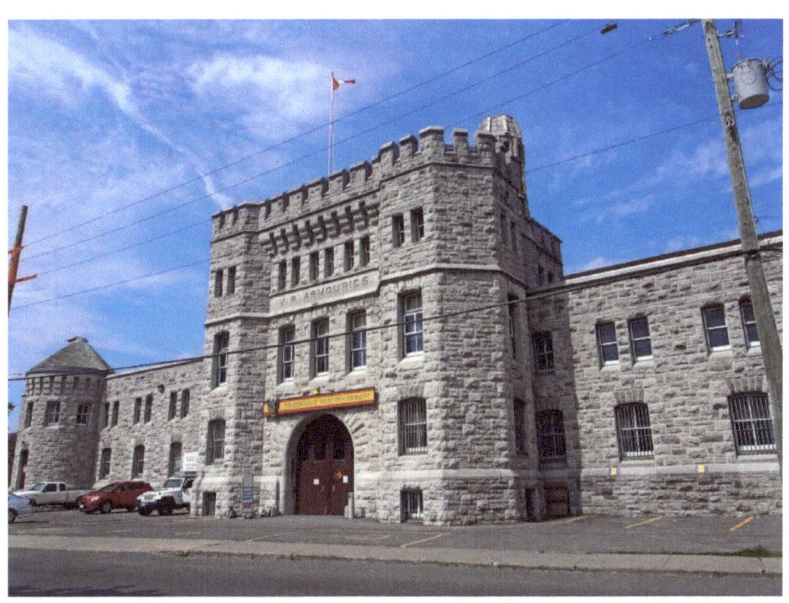

100 Montreal Street – Armouries, also known as the Kingston Drill Hall, is a two-storey, heavy stone structure. A long principal façade articulated by a prominent three-storey projecting frontispiece, serves as the main entrance and consists of a troop door and two flanking stair towers. There are two rows of evenly spaced, deeply set windows along the long wall, crenels across the frontispiece, and large decorative corbels around the side towers.

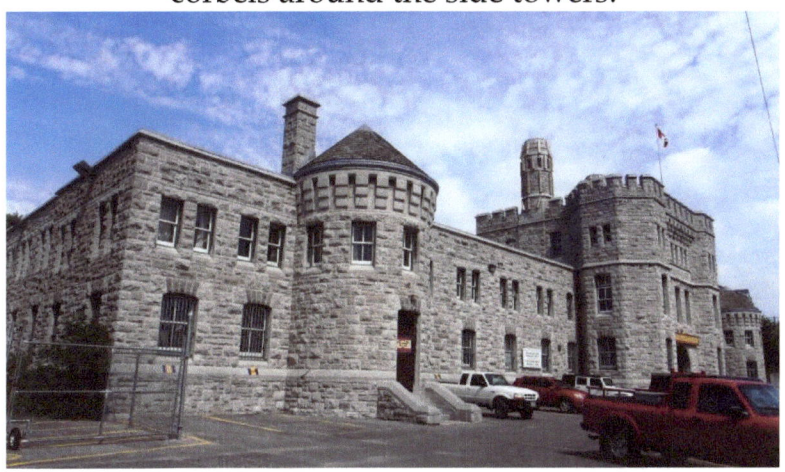

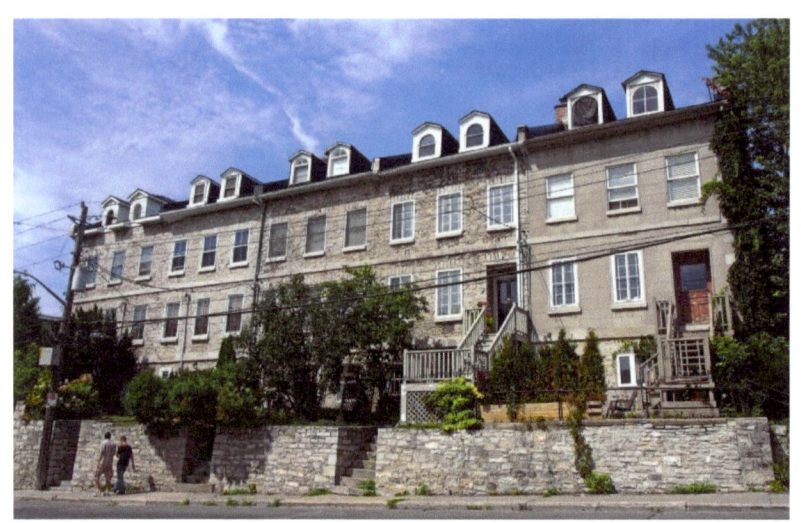

Montreal Street - dormers

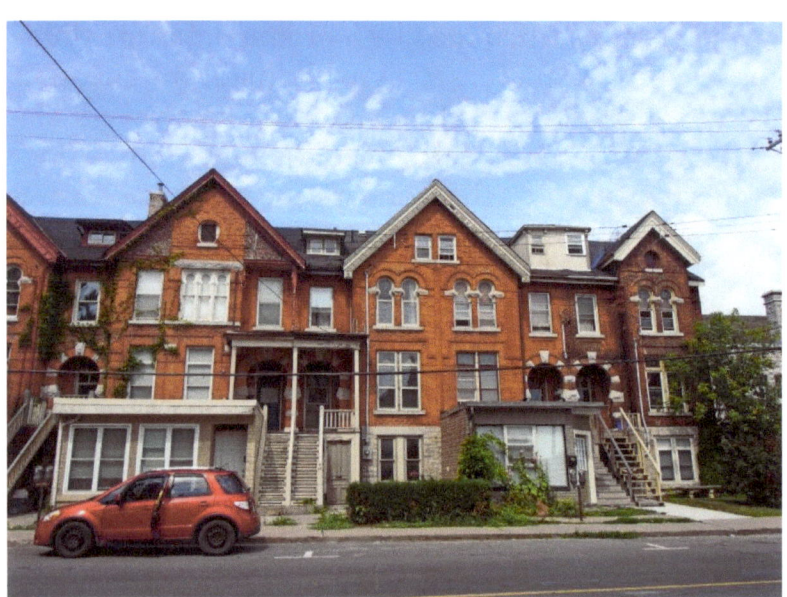

60-72 Montreal Street – Gothic Revival, voussoirs, keystones, dormers

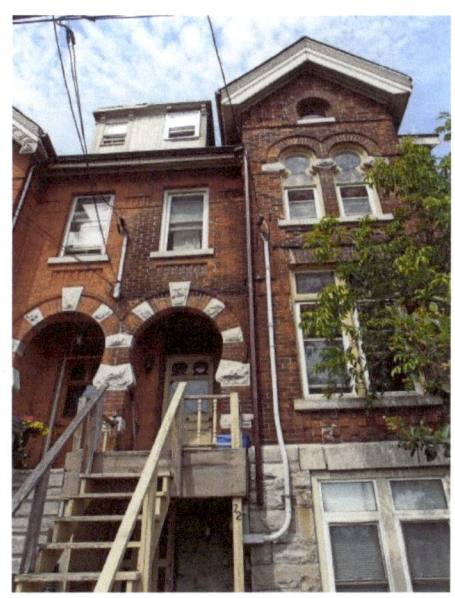

72 Montreal Street – dichromatic stone and brick voussoirs

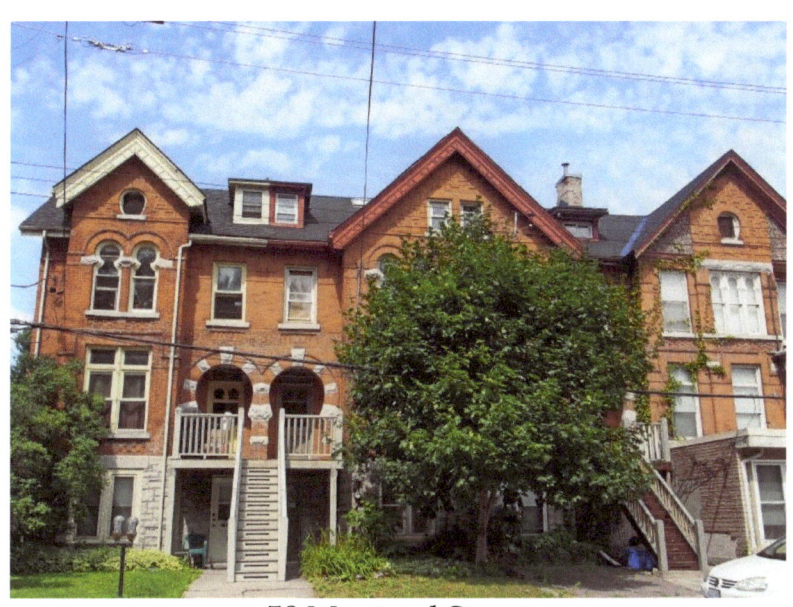

50 Montreal Street

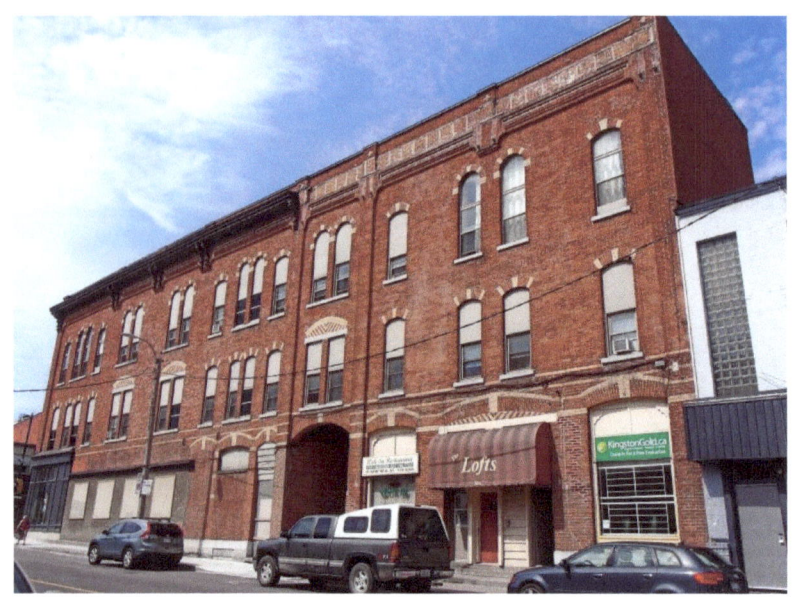

Montreal Street – three-storey red brick, dichromatic
brickwork, dentil moulding, pilaster

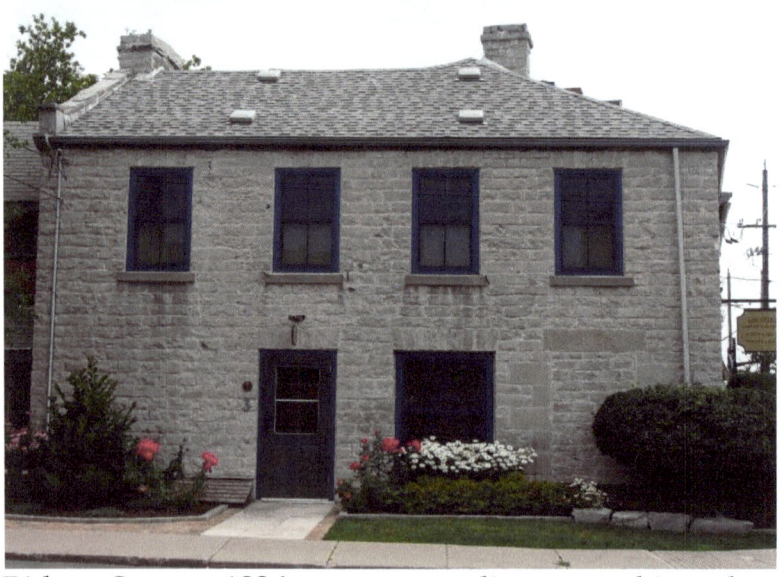

3 Rideau Street – 1826 – two storey limestone, hipped roof

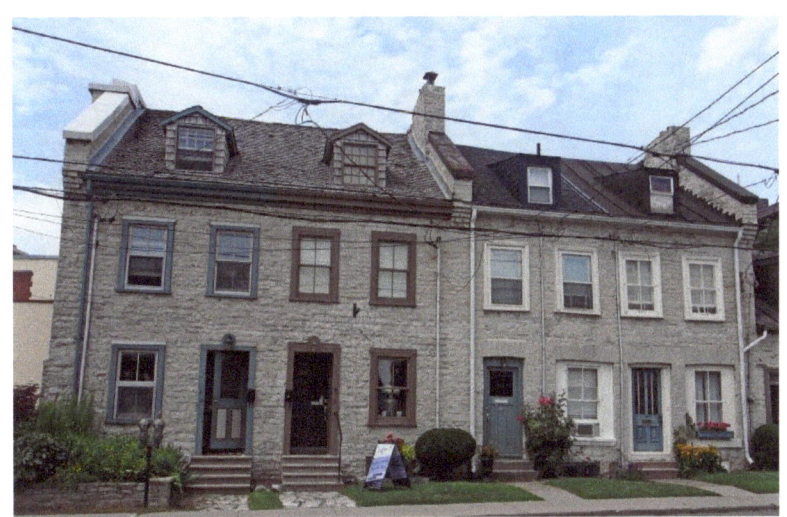

6-12 Rideau Street – two-storey limestone, dormers

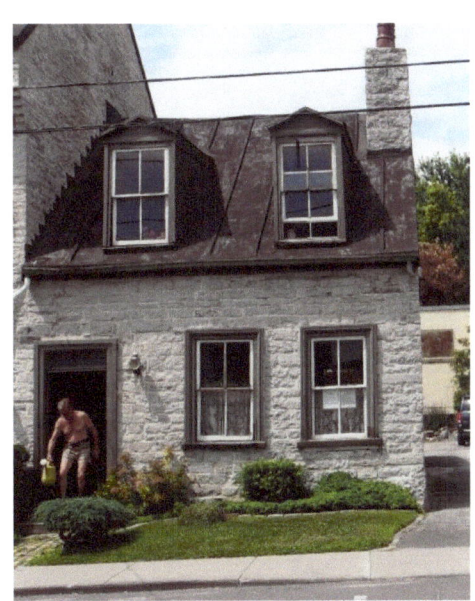

14 Rideau Street – one-storey limestone, dormers

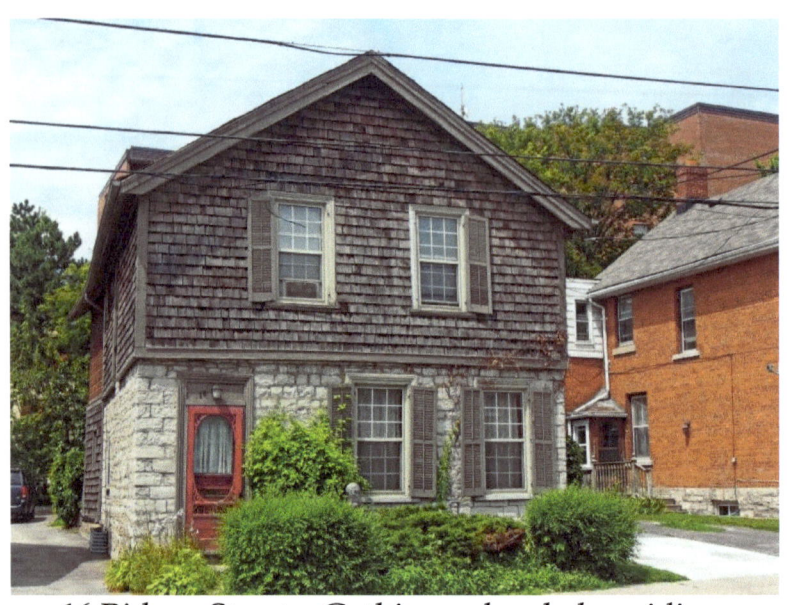

16 Rideau Street – Gothic - cedar shakes siding,
9-over-9 sash windows

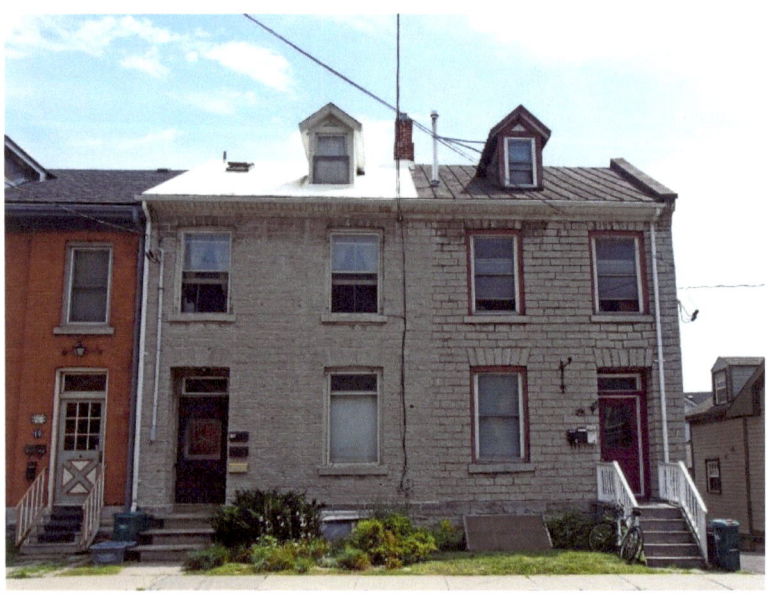

15-17 Rideau Street – two storey limestone, dormers

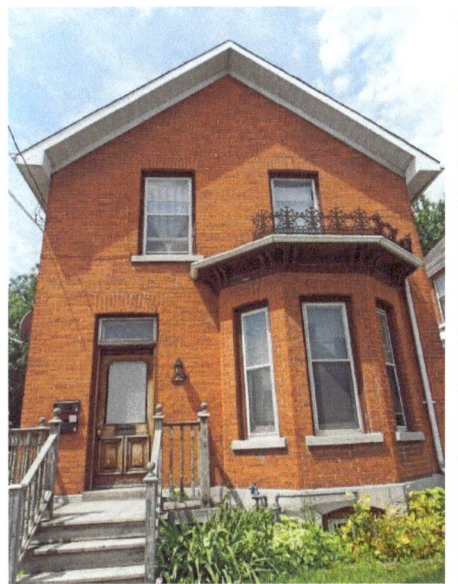

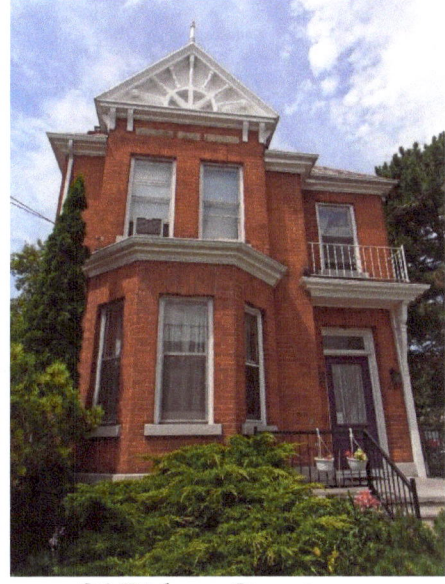

20 Rideau Street
Gothic Revival, bay window,
Iron cresting

26 Rideau Street
2-storey tower-like bay,
pediment, cornice brackets

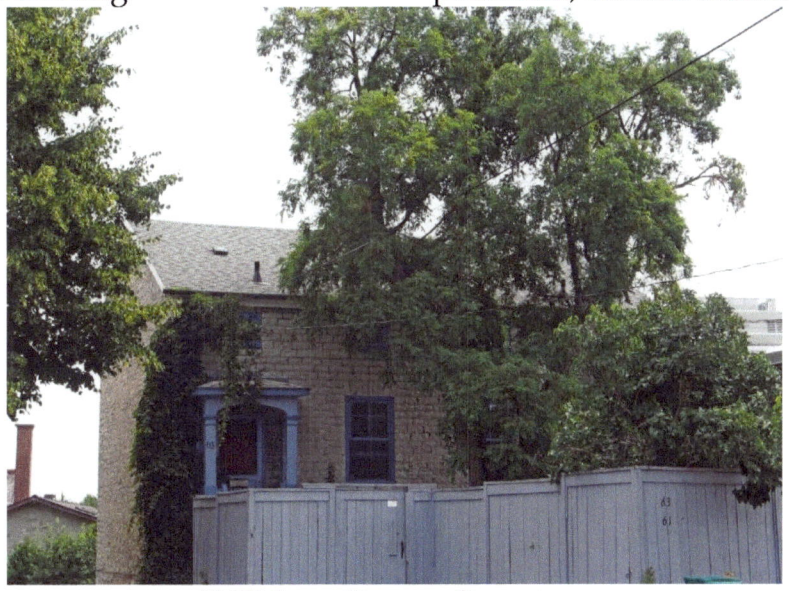

63 Rideau Street – limestone

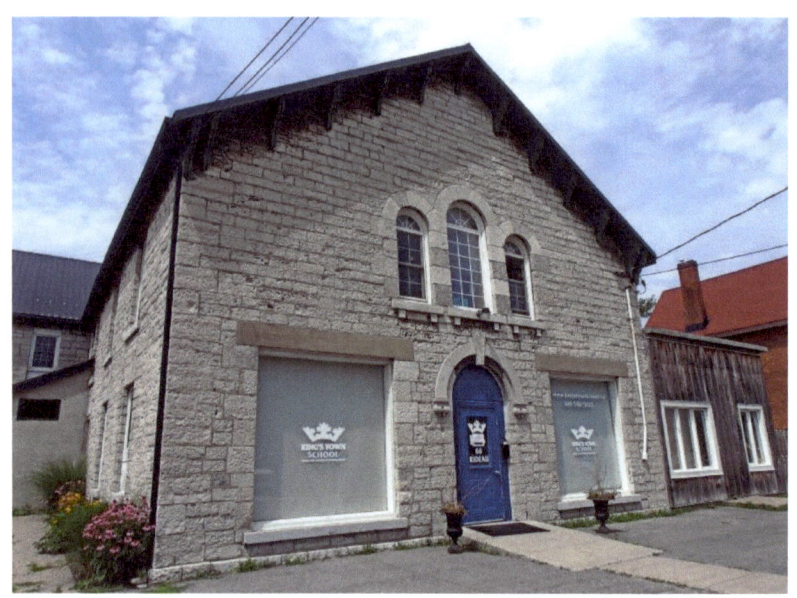

66 Rideau Street - limestone

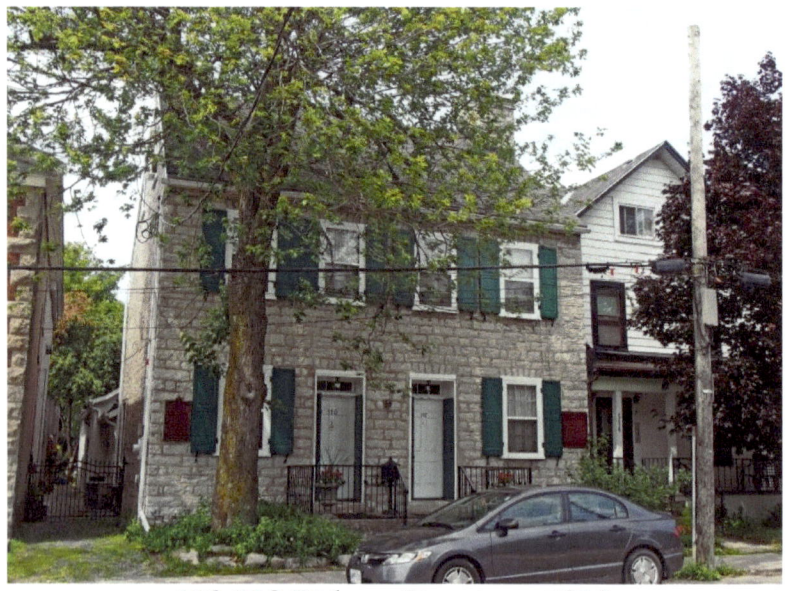

110-112 Rideau Street – c. 1810

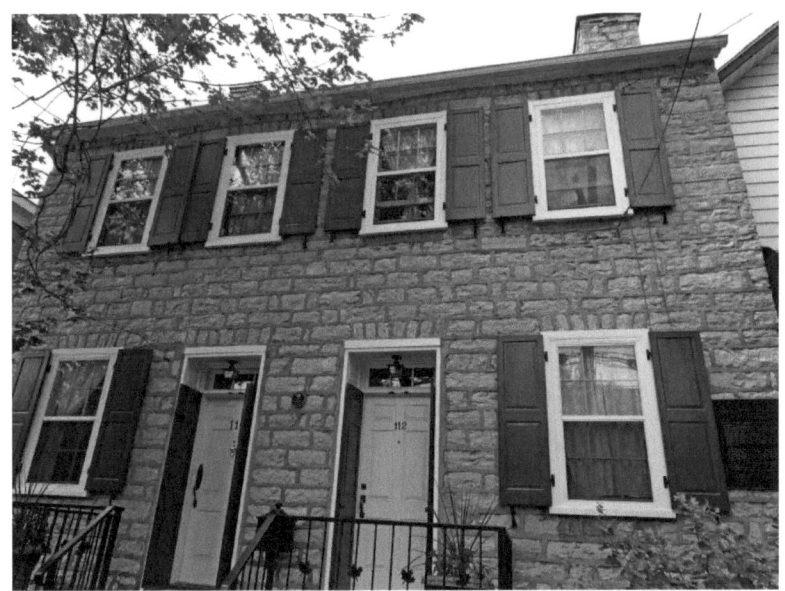

110-112 Rideau Street – two-storey limestone

Sir John A. MacDonald, Statesman and Patriot, spent his boyhood days, 1835-1839, those years that decide the character of the man, were spent here in the Old Town which has seen more than a century of Canadian History.

Born in Scotland, Sir John A. MacDonald, with his superb skills remained at the centre of public life for fifty years. The political genius of Confederation, he became Canada's first prime minister in 1867, held that office for nineteen years (1867-73, and 1878-91), and presided over the expansion of Canada to its present boundaries excluding Newfoundland. His National Policy and the building of CPR were equally indicative of his determination to resist the north-south pull of geography and to create and preserve a strong country politically free and commercially autonomous.

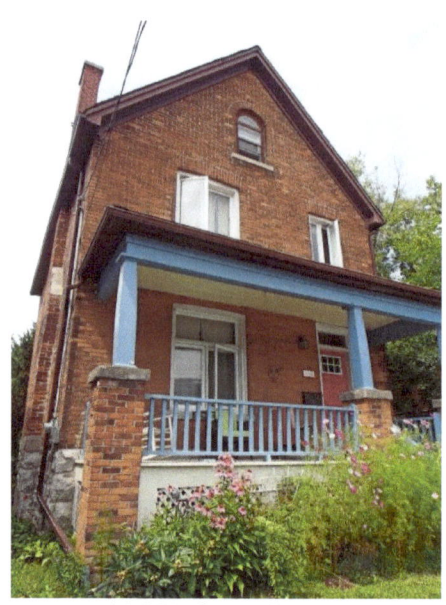

116 Rideau Street

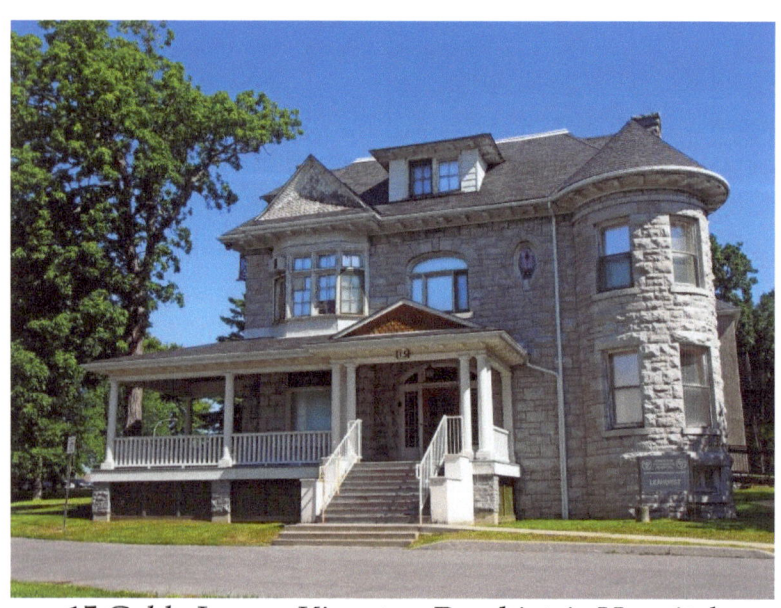

15 Gable Lane – Kingston Psychiatric Hospital

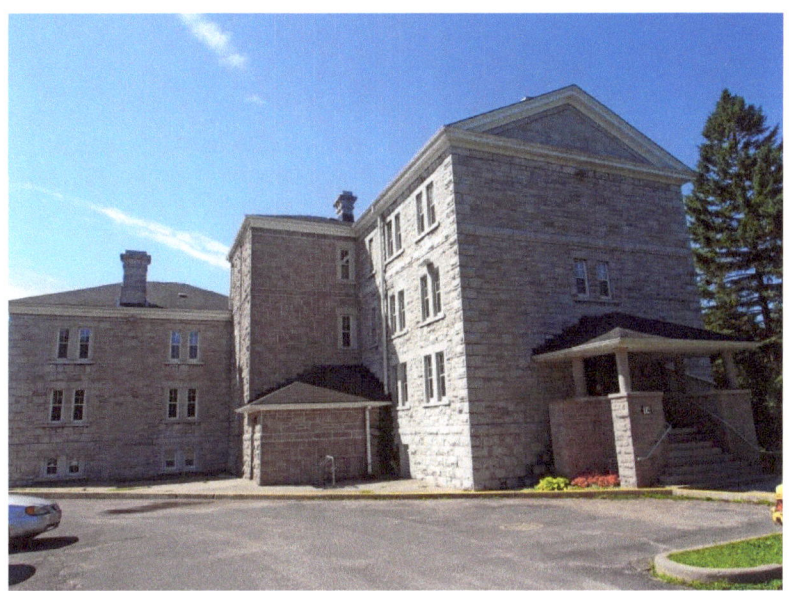

Heakes Lane

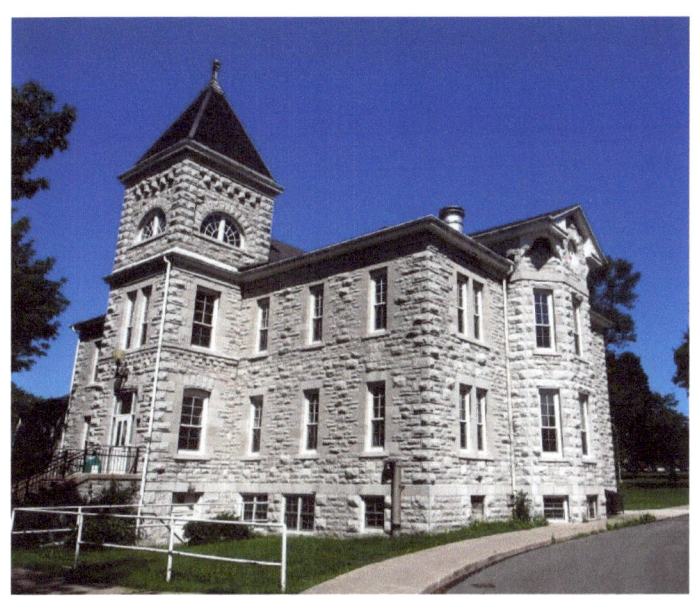

Beechgrove Cottage – built in 1893 with a 1914 addition - part
of the Rockwood Insane Asylum complex to house patients
with acute diseases and as a convalescent home

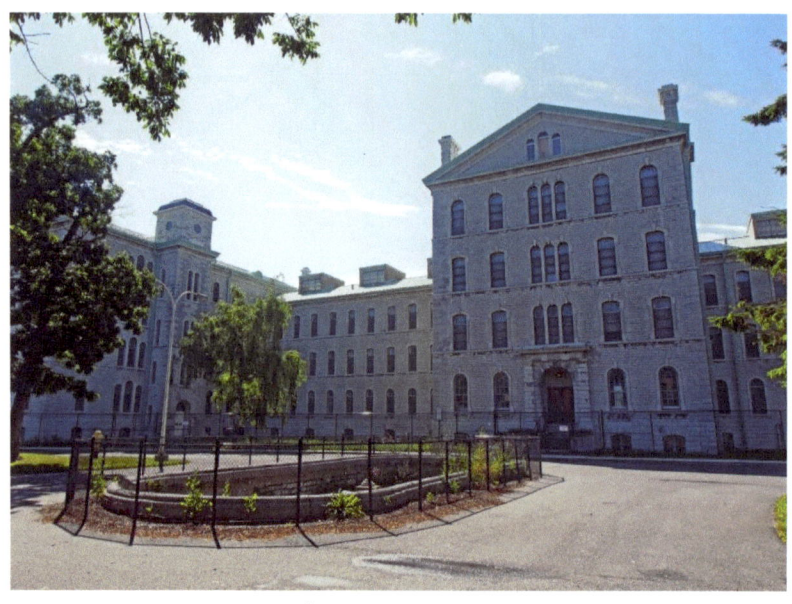

Gable Lane – Construction, by convict labor from the nearby Kingston Penitentiary, of The Rockwood Lunatic Asylum for the Criminally Insane commenced in 1859, was completed by 1870 with its first patients moving in as early as 1862. Architect William Coverdale designed the building, with rooms nine feet by nine feet, larger windows and more substantial common areas. It also had Canada's first central heating plant, installed as a safety measure to eliminate potential fire issues. Renamed Penrose sometime in the 1900s the institution was closed in 2000.

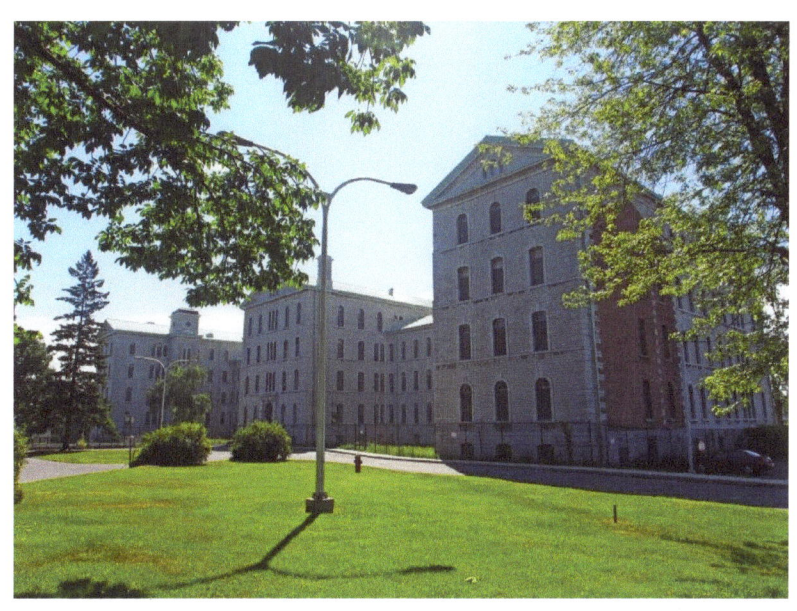

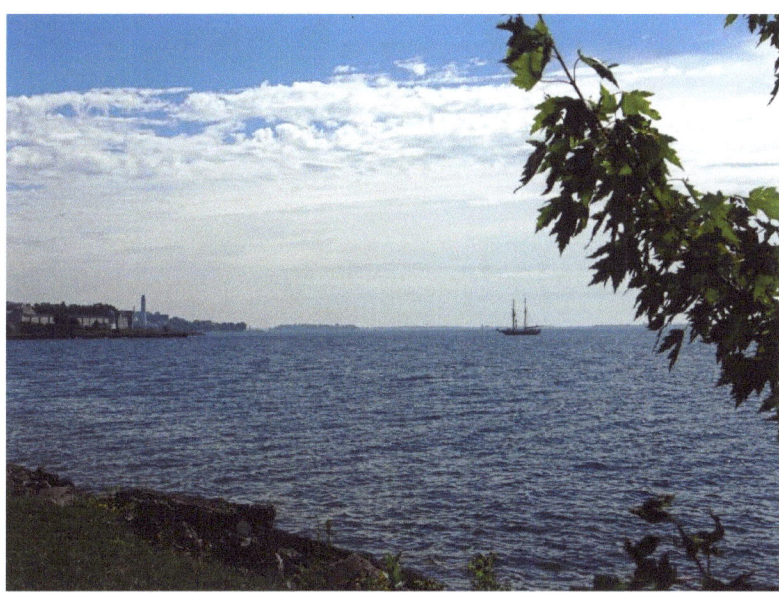

Lake Ontario

Bay Window: A window that projects out from a wall, in a semicircular, rectangular, or polygonal design. Used frequently in Gothic and Victorian designs. Example: 200 Union Street, Page 24	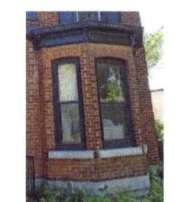
Belvedere: (from the Italian "beautiful view") an architectural feature on a roof, in a garden or on a terrace that gives a beautiful view. Example: 371 King Street West, Page 11	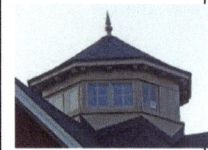
Brackets: a decorative or weight-bearing structural element which forms a right angle with one side against a wall and the other under a projecting surface such as an eave or roof. Example: 82 Lower Union Street, Page 31	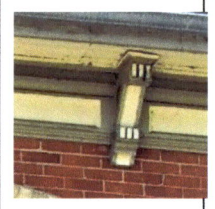
Buttress: a masonry structure built against or projecting from a wall which serves to support or reinforce the wall. In Canadian architecture, they are sometimes used for decoration. Example: Union Street, Page 26	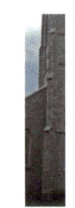

Capital: The uppermost finish or decoration on a column. A Doric column is characterized by a plain column with no base, a shaft with twenty flutings, and a simple capital with a simple entablature. Example: 81 Lower Union Street, Page 24 A Corinthian column is characterized by a rounded capital decorated with acanthus leaves and a square abacus (the uppermost portion of a capital directly below the entablature) on tall slender columns. Example: 163 Union Street, Page 22	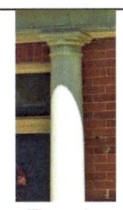 Doric 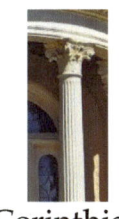 Corinthian
Cornice: originally the wooden overhang of the roof. With the use of stone, brick, iron and steel, the cornice is any projecting shelf at the top of a ceiling or roof. They can be very decorative. Example: Union Street, Page 20	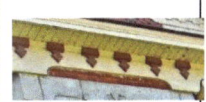
Cornice Return: decorative element on the end of a gable. Example: Union Street, Page 25	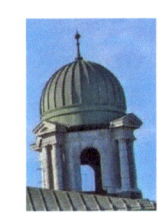
Cupola: A domed or curved roof rising from a building as a decorative element. Example: Women's Penitentiary, Page 10	

Dentil Moulding: an even series of rectangles used as ornamental decoration in cornices. Example: Union Street, Page 21	 Bevelled
Dichromatic brickwork: the use of two colours of brick, tile or slate to decorate a façade. Example: 82 Lower Union Street, Page 31	
Dormer: (French for "sleep") a gable end window that pierces through the plane of a sloping roof surface to create usable space in the top floor or attic of a building by adding headroom. Example: 1212 Woodbine Road, Page 20	
Frontispiece: a portion of the façade of a building, usually a centred doorway that is slightly raised from the rest of the building, usually has extensive ornamentation. Frontispieces are usually Classical in design with white columned porches. Example: King Street West, Page 10	
Gable: the triangular portion of a wall between the edges of a sloping roof. **Jacobean Gable:** the gable extends above the roofline. Example: 462 King Street West, Page 14	
Hipped Roof: a roof where all sides slope downwards to the walls with no gables. Example: 163 Union Street, Page 22	

Iron Cresting: A decorative ornament along the top of a roof. Iron cresting was popular in the Baroque era and also in Italianate, Victorian, Second Empire and Queen Anne styles of architecture. Example: 20 Rideau Street, Page 47	
Keystones and Voussoirs: a voussoir is a wedge-shaped element used in building an arch. A keystone is the central stone that locks all the stones into position, allowing the arch to bear weight. A keystone is often enlarged and embellished. Example: 60-72 Montreal Street, Page 42	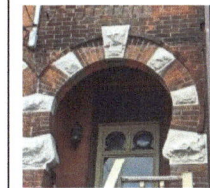
Lancet Window: a tall, narrow window with a pointed arch at its top. Example: King Street West, Page 12	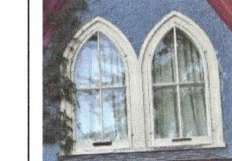
Mansard Roof: This style was popularized by Francois Mansart (1598-1666), an accomplished architect of the French Baroque period and especially fashionable during the Second French Empire (1852-1870). This roof is almost flat on the top section, with two slopes on each of its sides with the lower slope at a steeper angle than the upper and having dormer windows. Example: 99-101 Lower Union Street, Page 32	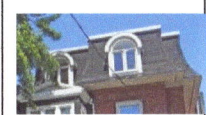
Pediment: a triangular section above the horizontal structure (entablature), typically supported by columns. The inside of the triangle is called the tympanum. Example: 26 Rideau Street, Page 46	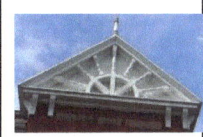

Pilaster: a slightly projecting column built into or applied to the face of a wall for additional structural support. Example: Montreal Street, Page 44	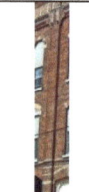
The **quatrefoil** is a type of decorative framework consisting of a symmetrical shape which forms the outline of four partially overlapping circles of the same diameter. The word quatrefoil comes from Latin and means "four leaves". Example: Ordnance Street, Page 39	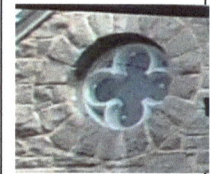
Quoin: masonry blocks at the corner of a wall, often a decorative feature, usually larger or of a different colour than the rest of the wall. Example: 111 Lower Union Street, Page 34	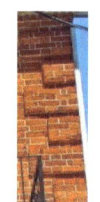
Sidelight: a window, usually with a vertical emphasis, that flanks a door, and is often used to emphasize the importance of a primary entrance. **Transom Window:** the light above the doorway, also called a fanlight. Example: 163 Union Street, Page 22	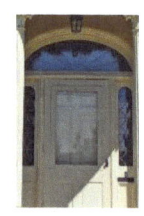
Verge board and Finial: also called bargeboards – hang from the projecting end of a roof and are often elaborately carved and ornamented. **Finial:** ornament added to the top of a gable, pinnacle, canopy or spire – a Gothic element. Example: Lower Union Street, Page 29	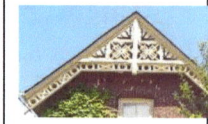

Building Styles

Gothic Revival, 1830-1890 – These decorative buildings have sharply-pitched gables with highly detailed verge boards, pointed-arch window openings, and dichromatic brickwork. It is a common style in Ontario. Example: 81 Lower Union Street, Page 31	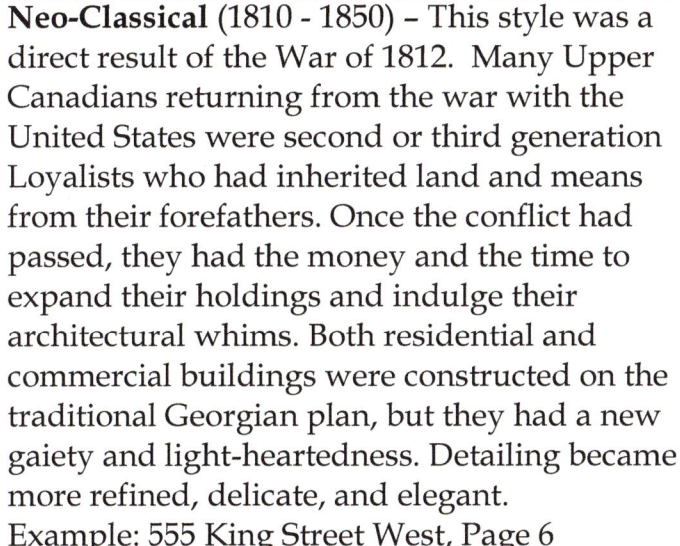
Italianate, 1850-1900 – A two story rectangular building with a mild hip roof, a projecting frontispiece, and generous eaves with ornate cornice brackets was the basis of the style; often there are large sash windows, quoins, ornate detailing on the windows, belvederes and wraparound verandahs. Italianate commercial buildings often have cast iron cresting and elegant window surrounds. Example: 82 Lower Union Street, Page 31	
Neo-Classical (1810 - 1850) – This style was a direct result of the War of 1812. Many Upper Canadians returning from the war with the United States were second or third generation Loyalists who had inherited land and means from their forefathers. Once the conflict had passed, they had the money and the time to expand their holdings and indulge their architectural whims. Both residential and commercial buildings were constructed on the traditional Georgian plan, but they had a new gaiety and light-heartedness. Detailing became more refined, delicate, and elegant. Example: 555 King Street West, Page 6	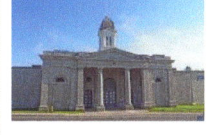

Regency Cottage, 1830-1860 – This style originated in England in 1815 and spread to Ontario later in the 19th century as British officers retired to Canada. It is a modest one-storey house with a low-pitched hip roof and has a symmetrical front façade. Example: 56 King Street West, Page 15	
Romanesque Revival, 1880-1910 – This style hearkens back to medieval architecture of the 11th and 12th centuries with a heavy appearance, blocky towers and rounded arches. Example: Ordnance Street, Page 39	
Second Empire, 1860-1880 – The mansard roof is the most noteworthy feature of this style and is evidence of the French origins. Projecting central towers and one or two-storey bays can also be present. Example: 169 Union Street, Page	
Tudor Revival – exposed timbers with stucco infill, multi-paned windows. Example: King Street West, Page 11	

www.ingramcontent.com/pod-product-compliance
Lightning Source LLC
Chambersburg PA
CBHW040849180526
45159CB00001B/370